THE
Granny-Nanny

A Guide For Parents & Grandparents
Who Share Child Care

By Lee Edwards Benning

THE
Granny-Nanny

A Guide For Parents & Grandparents Who Share Child Care

Cleveland Clinic Press/January 2006
All rights reserved
Copyright © Lee Edwards Benning

Contact:
Cleveland Clinic Press
9500 Euclid Ave. NA32
Cleveland, OH 44195
216-444-1158
chilnil@ccf.org
www.clevelandclinicpress.org

Any medical information in this book is not intended to replace personal medical care and supervision; there is no substitute for the experience and information that your doctor can provide. Rather, it is our hope that this book will provide additional information to help family members who share child care.

Proper medical care should always be tailored to the individual patient. If you read something in this book that seems to conflict with your doctor's instructions, contact your doctor. Since each individual case differs, there may be good reasons for individual treatment to differ from the information presented in this book.

If you have any questions about any treatment in this book, consult your doctor.

ISBN: 1-59624-003-2

Library of Congress Control Number: 2005933059

Cover and Book Design: Whitney Campbell & Co. • Advertising & Design

This book is dedicated

to my fellow Granny-Nanny,

Arthur E. Benning, Sr.,

who loves, hugs, feeds, even diaper-changes,

not to mention writing and editing

And to those youngsters

from whom we learned so much:

Emma Paris, Paige Amanda, and Tara Sophia Benning

as well as

Dawn, Julio, Nathalie, Melissa, and Tommy

And to the 79 percent of grandparents out there

who, according to one survey,

pitch in each year to help care for their grandchildren

Good for you!

CONTENTS

CONTENTS

What's A Granny-Nanny?

gran·ny – nan·ny \\'gra-nē-'na-nē\ *n., pl.* granny-nannies.

1. A phrase combining an abbreviation with a (chiefly Brit.) word of baby-talk origin

2. A grandparent who provides child care on a daily or temporary basis, sometimes known as "relative care" (syn: parent-in-a-pinch; maternal [or paternal] nursemaid; savior; easy-touch; best and lovingest care giver any grandchild could have)

3. Old female goat (syn: granny-nanny-goat; granny who won't play nanny)

Notes To A Fellow Grandparent, Be You A He Or A She

You're Thinking Of Granny-Nannying? Lucky you!

Who says opportunity only knocks once? Don't believe it. If given the privilege—and I do consider it a privilege, not a chore—of caring for a grandchild, you are being given a second chance. At what? At parenting! That's what, and that's unusual.

Yes, I Mean You, Too, Pops

There are a lot more grandfathers out there Granny-Nannying than you might think. And why not? You are admirably suited for the job: all the mentoring you have done out in your earlier work life has prepared you for the task. You are, of course, a natural for older boys—better than any Nana will be—but you'll be surprised at how good you are with infants. Forget about that diapering business (with disposables it's a cinch) . . . and preparing formulas (just add water to powder) . . . and sterilizing (hello, dishwasher!). Granny-Nannying of infants comes down essentially to one thing: patience. It also helps to be a little hard of hearing during teething times. So, just because you don't happen to be of the traditional Granny-Nanny gender, don't pass up an opportunity of a lifetime. Step up to the plate, and volunteer!

Sure, more obvious and mundane considerations (like helping the kids out financially) may enter into your decision. What will make it special is finally experiencing all the firsts you missed the first time.

Most likely the first time around, you, like me, were busy with a new spouse, a new home, a new career. Your time was limited. The day never seemed to have enough minutes in it.

Looking back you may have experienced more than one guilt trip. A time when you were torn between a child's needs and someone else's, and your child took second place. Here's your chance to make up in a small way for those gaffes. Now, finally, when your children are grown, you have time. Lots of time. Maybe more time than you may know what to do with. Which makes you the perfect candidate for Granny-Nannydom!

Now there's time, if your back permits, for you to hand-walk a toddler round and round the house as he takes his first baby steps. Or read for the umpteenth time a children's book. (I recommend Peggy Rathmann's *Ten Minutes to Bedtime*. Unlike many, it does not grow stale on repetition.)

Now you not only have the opportunity but also the time to attend every school performance, every religious pageant, every dance or music recital, every sporting event. When you discover what you missed the first time around, you may want to kick yourself . . . but don't. Let's face it, back then you didn't have any other choice, any more than today's parents do.

One of the greatest gifts you will receive is being a witness to your own immortality. You will see some of your own childrearing techniques being passed on to the next generation. For example, the other night, my granddaughter asked to be excused from the table on the basis that she was full. To my surprise, her mother said, "Let me check your tummy." Up went the blouse, a gentle hand prodded the tummy, then a motherly voice confided, "Oh, my, I do believe there's a hole over here. One large enough for at least two more bites." As my grandchild sat down willingly to eat those two bites, I had to swallow hard myself. That was a technique I had used twenty some years ago! Pride, get ye behind me!

Taking care of your grandchildren is like being a parent all over again—only this time you have the time to enjoy it. You know the tricks that worked the first time, and those that didn't. You are experienced. You won't go through all the troubles and travails of the first childrearing.

Why Did I Write This Book?

Why did I write the book? Because I'm a book person. Faced with anything new, I look for a book on the subject. And I was frustrated because there wasn't anything out there that would tell me what I was agreeing to when I said I'd be a Granny-Nanny. Oh, sure, there were books on how to be a long-distance grandmother or a full-time parental grandmother, but not a shared-care giver.

I hoped that through it, I could share what I've learned. Reassure like-minded Granny-Nannies and parents that things can and will work out. Coax and convince reluctant ones that this is an opportunity they should grab. Alert everyone to little problems before they became big ones.

In other words, to put it bluntly, I saw a need and thought I had the background, the credentials, and the experience to fill it.

You can relax and know it will all turn out well in the end. So, she's not potty trained at three. She will be eventually, all kids are. So, he has trouble counting to a hundred; when it comes to pennies, he'll learn real fast.

This doesn't mean you won't have house rules and set guidelines for conduct. All that smart-alecky business about spoiling a child and then sending him home to his parents doesn't work, not if you're Granny-Nannying. Guess what? Those spoiled brats will be back the next day or the next or the one after that.

To misquote Dr. Seuss, "Oh, the wonderful things a Granny-Nanny can do!" And the greatest experience of all is when a grandchild, without thinking, calls you Mommy or Daddy instead of Granny or Pops. And that can spell trouble.

Let's be frank, Daddy may laugh it off, but Mother isn't going to find it so funny. She's likely to have clenched lips, smoke belching out of her ears, and eyes shooting warning sparks. BEWARE! Mothers seem to feel—and rightly so—that no one can take their place. Fortunately, grandchildren have a way of smoothing out rough spots between parents and grandparents. For one thing, the children give you both something of mutual interest and equal concern to discuss.

To be truthful, one of the most difficult aspects of the situation is role reversal. Before, you were the alpha female, the queen bee in your household. Now the child's mother comes first. That can be hard to take, especially if that mother happens to be your daughter. But there are so many other compensations: being the first to post a drawing on the refrigerator . . . being the first to be told that Ryan is a dirty-dog but kind of cute . . . being the first to cheer a grandson's home run or goal.

If I make this sound like it's all peaches and cream, I'm not doing you a favor. It has its pitfalls. For one thing, you may have hobbies and outside interests you're going to have to postpone for a while or even give up. At least until the children are in school full-time.

For another, and this is a big one, your body is not what it used to be. Keeping up with energetic young ones can be physically exhausting.

But look at it this way:
Life should NOT be a journey to the grave with the intention of arriving safely in an attractive and well-preserved body, but rather one should skid in sideways, doll in one hand, baseball mitt in the other, body thoroughly used up and totally worn out, while screaming, "Oh, them kids! What a ride!"

A Word To The Parent, Whether You're On Your Own Or In A Partnership

You have a chance at getting a Granny-Nanny? Don't think twice! Grab it! And hold on tight!

A Granny-Nanny is the best thing all parents can have going, especially single parents. Much if not most of the work is done before you begin. No references to check. No settings to give the once-over. No concern over neglect. AND Granny-Nannying frequently comes with extras, such as: "Why don't you join us for dinner?" No child care center or au pair is going to offer that.

Having a Granny-Nanny will give your child the only thing money can't buy: love. You can go off each day knowing that your child or children will be cared for as if they were the Granny-Nanny's own—which in a sense they are.

There are so many advantages to this situation that it would take a book (like this one) to describe them.

Don't kid yourself, it won't be easy. You may find yourself in the position of admonishing an older woman because she isn't up on all the modern techniques. Wow, does that take tact! On the other hand, these are your children, not hers. Any halfway sensible Granny-Nanny will be well aware of this.

At times, you may resent that the Granny-Nanny gets to experience some of the firsts that you feel are your due. But a second telling sometimes just polishes the story.

And you may be pleasantly surprised to discover that your relationship with the Granny-Nanny has blossomed, and your entire family has benefited from the situation.

The many young parents I have surveyed have firmly convinced me that if a Granny-Nanny situation is available, grab it. Hold on to it. Do all you can to make it a success, and it will pay umpteen dividends.

However, you'll feel much more comfortable with your decision if you check out your other options. Believe you me, you will be far, far happier with your choice of a Granny-Nanny if you are aware of what else lurks out there.

Who's Minding
The Children Now?

The most recent survey of America's families tells us that, surprisingly enough, only 27 percent of children under age five are cared for the traditional way—by their parents. So, who's minding the rest of them?

- 4 percent of children under the age of five are taken care of by nannies.

- 28 percent of children under age five are cared for in group day cares and preschools.

- 14 percent are in family day care or a day care with between four and eight children.

- 6 percent are taken care of by relatives other than grandparents.

- And the remaining 21 percent of all children under the age of five are cared for on a regular basis by their grandparents.

PART I

Oh, The Wonderful Choices Parents Have

The American child care system, in which parents, largely unassisted, must buy the care they need in the marketplace, has not worked well.

—Susanne W. Helburn and Barbara R. Bergmann,

America's Child Care Problem

Perhaps that's the understatement of the decade.

Helburn and Bergmann's book, in addition to making suggestions on how to improve child care, does an excellent job of analyzing existing problems. I highly recommend it. The book goes on to quote a mother and child care user, Mary George. Ms. George, a journalist and writer, formerly with *The Denver Post*, said, "I found a 1995 study, 'Cost, Quality, and Child Care Centers,' that had disturbing, close-to-home information. ... They ranked the overall quality of child care in my state as mediocre and observed very few good quality centers ...

"But here's the fact that really floored me: Most of the care observed in the study was mediocre, but the vast majority of parents said their kids were getting excellent care."

Why bother researching other choices when you've already decided to use the services of a Granny-Nanny? Because you need a plan B, or backup plan. Suppose—God forbid—something happened to your Granny-Nanny? A fall, an illness, some major setback that made it impossible for her to sit or continue to sit? In the words of Tom Lehrer's "Boy Scouts' Marching Song"—BE PREPARED!

Although experts say that the number of children needing child care exceeds the number of accommodations by about five to one, parents still have some choices ... but it's a jungle out there, and competition is fierce. The key to finding what you want is to move fast. Which means starting to look the day your pregnancy strip tests positive. The one exception: if your employer offers child care —which we'll get into later.

Even though you're going to use a Granny-Nanny, just in case something happens, you should have at least an idea about what other options are available. And it may be that after checking these out, both pro and con, you might decide not to go the Granny-Nanny route at all.

CHAPTER 1

The Group Experience

"I walked into the room and thought I'd been
transported to Romania. It was lined wall to wall
with cribs. The room reeked of urine and was eerily silent.
Wide-eyed youngsters occupied every crib
with not a toy, much less a mobile, in sight.
One attendant sat in the middle of the room, an infant lying
across her lap as she burped it."

—A mother upon visiting the "infant" section of a large day care center

---

(Please note, nursery schools or preschools are not discussed in this section. They are not child care providers per se, but adjuncts to child care and educational in nature. Read more about them in Chapter 14, page 107.)

Day care! That's a parent's first thought. And no wonder. Day care facilities are growing like mushrooms all over the place—we have five new ones this year within two miles of our home. Not only that, schools, YMCAs, churches, and other organizations are starting them. Such new facilities offer convenience and are probably easiest to get into. Of course, it all comes at a price.

Child Care Centers

First, you need to find one that is not only licensed—and licensing requirements differ from state to state—but also accredited. Accreditation usually requires that the center meet higher standards than those required for licensing. (If you have your druthers, go for the center that is both accredited and licensed.) Accredited centers control group size, maintain small teacher-to-student ratios, especially for the youngest groups, and have snacks and/or meals that meet nutritional standards set by the Child Care Food Program of the U.S. Department of Agriculture. (For the seven major accrediting programs, see Appendix 6, page 219.)

There is considerable uniformity in approach and content of these accreditation groups, but the apparent similarities hide differences in general orientation, emphasis, and attention to detail. Standards vary in terms of staffing ratios, group size, teacher education qualifications, and in-service training.

Second, although it goes without saying that you need to visit any center that you are contemplating using, forget evening and weekend open houses. Here are major points to consider:

- You want to go while children are present. Yes, it's noisier. Yes, it's confusing. Yes, it's eye-opening.

- Take a sniff. Smell urine? Kiss the place good-bye.

- Where are the babies? Confined to cribs without crib toys for mental stimulation? That's not for you.

• Check the attendants. Are they rocking and hugging? How many of them are there? There should be a minimum of one for every six babies or infants.

• How long has the attendant who will be watching your child been employed there? As one mother who has worked at day care facilities noted, "Day cares have a huge turnover rate because of the horrible pay that these workers get, and because of this, it is not uncommon to have teachers that are inexperienced."

• Surreptitiously, look for runny noses. The biggest drawback by far of the child care center is disease. I don't care how often the attendants wash their hands, and with what, disease will always be a problem. In fact, according to the ARCH National Resource Center for Respite and Crisis Care (which began in 1991 as an initiative to promote respite services for families with children), "Because of their greater exposure to circulating diseases, infants and young children who spend time in group child care settings generally have a higher number of illnesses than those children cared for at home."

And that's just the beginning of the things you should look for. Most child care books cover the subject ad nauseam.

Church-Affiliated Day Care Centers

In most states, such facilities, because of their religious affiliation, are exempt from licensing. Some even avoid accreditation. Most are nursery schools, not child care facilities. Most—if they are good—are impossible to get into unless you are a member of the congregation and enroll your child at birth. Most are surprisingly hard to find; just check the Yellow Pages, most aren't in it. Most are very good, and relatively inexpensive (compared to commercial ones). Most won't let you deduct your child care costs as religious donations, but nice try! (More on this in Money Matters, page 99.)

Employer-Sponsored Child Care

The military child care system is by far the largest system of employer-sponsored child care and serves the largest percentage of employees. The only problem is that in order to take advantage of it one has to enlist in the armed services—which might be considered a rather drastic way to get child care. In civilian life there aren't that many employers sponsoring child care.

Availability of regular employer-supplied child care depends on how the service affects the company's bottom line. If, for example, there is a shortage of workers, as happened in the 1990s, employers see child care as a real benefit in getting and keeping employees.

Generally speaking, employer child care doesn't come cheap. For one thing, most such sites are contracted out to national firms that are in business to make a profit. Those that are run by the employer or by a parent board sitting in locus to the employer are at least break-even facilities. They may not make a profit, but they shouldn't lose money either—which most do if a great many infants are involved. For this reason, most employer child care centers use a sliding rate scale for enrollees: least for preschoolers, more for toddlers, most for infants—and some even impose a diaper charge.

Employer Child Care Pluses And Minuses

The advantages of these centers are many:

1. The convenience of the location. You go to work, you take your child with you. Many centers even allow parents to come visit on breaks; others don't.

2. The hours, which are roughly equivalent to the work force's hours.

3. Sick-child care is offered in some cases.

4. If a national contractor is running the center, standardized, formal policies exist as well as regional oversight, but most importantly, child care experience is part of the package.

The disadvantages of these centers are fewer but equally important:

1. As mentioned, they don't come cheap. Staff salaries are expected to be covered by fees. Many centers are on strict budgets when it comes to supplies. For example, one child care center, having used up its monthly supply budget, had to wait until the next month to get a $4.50 ream of paper for its copy machine. (The center's staff took up a collection.)

2. Part-time employees are usually expected to pay full-time fees, since staffing remains the same whether a child is there or not.

3. Child-to-staff ratios may be higher in some centers than in others to keep costs down.

4. Parent- or direct employer-run centers sometimes do not employ trained staff who know much about running a center, much less about how to provide the best child care.

5. When companies need to cut costs, such centers may be regarded as a drain on the bottom line, and so out they go.

Many parents, accepting that disease and child care centers go hand in hand, opt out of the group experience and decide to bring their child care provider into their home.

CHAPTER 2

The In-Home Experience

Take us on outings, give us treats. Sing songs, bring sweets.
Never be cross or cruel, never feed us castor oil, or gruel.
Love us as a son and daughter, and never smell of
barley water. …If you won't scold and dominate us,
we will never give you cause to hate us. We won't hide your
spectacles so you can't see, put toads in your bed,
or pepper your tea.

—Duties of a nanny, according to the children in *Mary Poppins*

Parents who choose to have their children cared for at home have a choice of five different types of caregivers, with some more difficult to find than others. The costs are relative—in some cases, taxes and Social Security payments must be made. Remember the famous "Nanny-Gate" that cost a potential Supreme Court justice her chance . . .

The easiest to find is

The Au Pair (translates literally as "the equal")

Once upon a time, this term referred to a student from abroad who came to this country to do light domestic work in exchange for room and board and a chance to learn colloquial English. Today, an au pair is a live-in foreign child care provider who is not supposed to do any light domestic work (some will make an exception, such as doing the dishes or the child's laundry).

To legally obtain an international au pair, the parent must hire one from a program authorized by the United States government.

Au pairs come to the United States for one year to provide up to forty-five hours of child care per week for their host family while pursuing educational credits. (Divide that by five days and you get nine hours of child care per day during the week and none on weekends or evenings. If you have an eight-hour workday, you've got thirty minutes each way for your commute.)

Those coming via the EduCare program (see page 220) provide up to thirty hours of child care a week. If you have a part-time job, this might work for you.

As conditions for hosting an exchange visitor under the au pair program, the government requires that you agree to:

1. Facilitate the enrollment and attendance of the au pair at an American "postsecondary" educational institution;

2. Ensure that the au pair has adequate transportation to attend that institution;

3. Pay the first $500 ($1,000 for EduCare participants) toward the costs of required academic course work. Any additional costs associated with acquiring the six academic credits (twelve for the EduCare participant) are to be absorbed by the au pair.

Translation: if the au pair is going to be sitting during the day for you, that person will be going to night school as well. So, no built-in babysitting.

If you thought going the au pair route was cheap, think again. The government estimates that the average annual cost, in 2004, to an American host family was about $13,000—which is typical government accounting and works only if your au pair doesn't eat or drink for the entire year or require a heated/air-conditioned room or need transportation anywhere.

The Bare Minimum

A typical fee schedule for au pairs procured from a licensed service in 2004 is:

Registration fee	$ 250
Placement fee	2,340
Program fee	2,900
52 weeks' salary	7,230
Educational cost	500
Subtotal	$13,220

Weekly wage is based on the minimum wage at the time; if it goes up, so does the total wage. Au pair wages are not usually subject to Social Security and Medicare taxes because of the au pair's status as a J-1 nonimmigrant and as a nonresident alien. Because the au pair's wages are paid for domestic service in a private home, they are not subject to U.S. income tax withholding and reporting on Forms 941 and W-2. However, au pair wages are includable in the gross income of the recipients, and au pairs are required to file U.S. individual income tax returns.

Then there is the slight matter of providing transportation (round-trip) from the arrival city to your home.

Moreover, au pairs are entitled to a private bedroom, all meals including weekends, one-and-one-half days off each week (providing the forty-five hours have not been used up during the week), a full weekend off each month, and two weeks of paid vacation.

Although you may pay them for extra child-sitting, one of your obligations as an au pair host is to see to it that the au pair has the opportunity to take advantage of cultural opportunities where you live, i.e., plan to act as tour guide for a while.

On the other hand, one of the great benefits of au pairs is that they are young, between eighteen and twenty-six. They have the energy to handle older children, preschoolers, and elementary students. In addition to perfecting their English, they can teach your child the rudiments of a foreign language (which is the reason French- or Spanish-speaking au pairs are preferred).

Besides those intangibles, before being placed with a host family, au pairs will receive at least eight hours of child safety and twenty-four hours of child development instruction. At least four hours of the child safety training will be infant-related, and at least four hours of the child development instruction will be devoted to the care of children under two years of age.

The child safety training, provided by qualified organizations, includes topics such as stress management, shaken baby syndrome, and CPR. Au pairs responsible for children under two years of age must have at least 200 hours of documented infant child care experience. Au pairs may not be placed with a family having a child less than three months of age unless a parent or other responsible adult is present in the home.

Au pairs will NOT have specialized training in nursing. They are NOT to provide child care services relating to the care and protection of infants and children, as would be performed by trained personnel such as registered or practical nurses. You can ask to see the results of a TB test (which is a legal necessity in some states), but you cannot ask if they have HIV, syphilis, or hepatitis.

Are you getting a pig in a poke when you sign up with such a service? In a sense, yes. The agency you use will screen the applicants, and you get to telephone-interview the applicant, but that doesn't guarantee that you will enjoy living with your au pair for weeks on end. Or vice versa. One family went through five au pairs in the first two years (two got homesick, one they couldn't deal with, one couldn't deal with them). And when they found a winner, they could not keep her for more than one year.

The family noted that several of their au pairs saw this trip abroad as a way to escape strict parental supervision and live it up a bit. That went against the family's own values.

Almost every book on child care deals, sometimes exhaustively, with the subject of au pairs. If you are seriously considering this option, I suggest you read one or more general child care books that will guide you in the process of obtaining one.

The Professional Nanny Or Governess

A status symbol for many, a necessity for others—especially those who work irregular hours or travel a great deal. Unfortunately, according to the International Nanny Association, demand exceeds supply by more than 25 percent.

Despite all the historical romances you may have read, education is the difference between a nanny and a governess, according to Jennifer Caccamo, of the English Nanny & Governess School in Ohio. A nanny has a high school education, a governess is college-educated.

Unlike the au pair, a young foreign student who works no more than forty-five hours a week and for one year only, the nanny is, or should be, a professional in that she has had some training, preferably at a nanny school. She can work more hours a week, and you can keep her for as long as you and she agree. She even has a week named in her honor, "The National Nanny Recognition Week," which in 2005 ran from September 25 to October 1.

The International Nanny Association defines the nanny as an individual "employed by a family on either a live-in or live-out basis to undertake all tasks related to the care of children. Duties are generally restricted to child care and the domestic tasks related to child care...Nanny's workweek ranges from forty to sixty hours per week. Usually works unsupervised."

Nannies vary in age and experience. There has been a marked increase in the last decade in the number of professional nannies, who have chosen the field as a career, not as a temporary stopgap while they decide on college, other work, or different options.

An entry-level live-out nanny will expect a minimum of $275 gross per week. Pay for a live-in nanny can range from $700 a week gross to over $1,000 and even higher for college-graduate-level or experienced nannies. Recognizing the key role geography plays in live-out wages, a nanny will command one-and-a-half to two times the minimum wage in less costly areas and upward of three to even four times the minimum wage in major metro markets. Experienced caregivers for infants and for more than two children generally command a premium.

Books on the subject allocate most of their space to the hunt for, interviewing of, and actual hiring of the caregiver. One book, the second most popular nanny book on Amazon.com, *The Complete Nanny Guide* by Cora Hilton Thomas, has as its subtitle *Solutions to Parents' Questions About Hiring and Keeping an In-Home Caregiver*. It devotes 96 percent of its pages, including eighteen appendices, to hiring the nanny, and 4 percent to how to keep that nanny.

That should give you some perspective on the difficulties of finding a nanny. The reasoning being: if you can't find one, you don't have to worry about keeping her.

Even harder to find is that combination cleaning-woman/child care provider:

The Housekeeper

Remember, even Mary Poppins didn't do dishes or run the vacuum. So, if you do find such a treasure, pinch yourself to make sure you're not dreaming. Compared with finding any other form of in-home care, this is the most desirable and most elusive. It is also the most expensive, other than a live-in medically trained nurse.

A housekeeper commands $10 to $20 an hour for housekeeping alone. Tack on another $5 to $10 if you want her to act as surrogate mommy.

Why so much? My question is why so little? How much do you think your own housekeeping and child care are worth? According to a UNICEF publication, "The value of women's *unpaid* subsistence and household work worldwide was estimated to be $11 trillion in 1995, nearly half the $23 trillion value of the world's total output of goods and services." Which is all well and good but how does it apply to individuals? Based on the *UK 2000 Time Use Survey*, released by the Office for National Statistics, it is estimated that if you are a stay-at-home houseperson, the value of your work in the household is worth between $904 and $1,085 per week in 2000 dollars. Work it out: If someone else did what you do, you'd pay between $47,023 and $56,416 a year. And that's for a forty-hour work week, not twenty-four/seven service with little or no time off and certainly no paid get-away-from-it-all vacations.

Not only are there few housekeepers around, but also you must compete with industry for them. And industry can provide benefits that the average family can't, such as life insurance, health care, overtime, and work shifts, meaning at the end of her shift she goes home. Not so easy in a household when the parents are delayed on their way home.

There are occasions when a more specialized type of in-home care is required:

A Real, Live Nurse

If your family situation is such that you need a specialized nurse, begin your search with American Nurses Association (ANA) in Washington, D.C. Or, if you have to deal with a situation such as cystic fibrosis or leukemia or kidney failure, you may be able to locate a specialized helper through a local chapter of one of the disease associations. Again there is a shortage of nurses, and again you will be competing with hospitals and the like for the services of the few registered nurses (RNs) available.

There are all sorts of advantages and no disadvantages to having a nurse in such a life-threatening situation. But looming large, there is the financial factor. RNs and even licensed practical nurses (LPNs) do not come cheap. However, it is quite possible that your health care provider, if you have one, or the state will help pick up the costs.

The most common in-home care provider is:

A Mother's Helper

She (although sometimes it might be a he) may be the perfect solution for the work-at-home parent or the parent of an older child. A mother's helper, whether in high school or college, is simply a glorified babysitter, but a definite improvement on having a latch-key kid. (Definition: child who has a house key—sometimes worn on a chain around the neck—to open the front door and return each day to an empty house.)

The mother's helper has little or no child care training (some of which you should insist on, such as basic first aid and CPR). If you plan to have her run errands or pick up the kids in a car, it goes without saying that she should have a valid driver's license and automobile insurance. But go one step farther and give her your own driving test. For example, have her actually drive to the school, see how she reacts to potential dangers, distractions, and so on. Take her to corners where you know there are problems; see how she handles them.

She should not be unsupervised for more than two hours at most. Which means she is only of value (and that can be tremendous) to the woman who works at home or gets home shortly after the kids do. Mother's helpers sometimes will perform light chores such as loading the dishwasher or picking up after the kids —it's up to the family to negotiate. She is, in a sense, a space holder—someone responsible to fill in between school and parental arrival.

A mother's helper is relatively inexpensive, with a salary range from $65 to $100 a week. If she is needed for short periods of time, she will probably charge a minimum fee of $20 to $25. Figure an hourly rate of between $6 and $7 an hour, but in some areas it will be much higher.

How do you find such an angel? Through local youth groups and churches, advertisements in your neighborhood paper, word of mouth.

Some mother's helpers actually live in, in which case they are the American equivalents of au pairs. However, their average workday is ten hours, five days a week, which includes the time the children are in school. A mother's helper usually gets holidays and weekends off and is on flex time, i.e., free time or time off in lieu of overtime. Normally she has the use of a car (check your auto insurance and her license) to run errands, but some families give her the use of the car at any time. She is treated like one of the family and has her own room and travels with the family.

A live-out mother's helper works a minimum of four hours per day and costs between $6 and $10 per hour. She will receive most of the benefits of a live-in mother's helper except the private room and twenty-four/seven use of the car. For the sake of neighborhood tranquillity, think long and hard before you hire a neighbor's daughter as your mother's helper. If she doesn't work out, firing her is easier said than done.

CHAPTER 3

Family And Friends

The use of extended family and clan care in Ireland
can be traced back to life under the Brehon laws
(Irish native laws, circa 300AD to mid-1600s).

—Seamus O'hInnse, *Miscellaneous Irish Annals (A.D. 1114-1437)*

Call it a clan, call it a network, call it a tribe,
call it a family. Whatever you call it, whoever you are,
you need one.

—Jane Howard

Generally speaking, this is where most parents turn. Sometimes because they can't find anything else. Sometimes because they can't get their first (or second) choice. Sometimes because it is more convenient and less expensive than almost anything else.

Home Day Care, a.k.a. Family Day Care

Both are misnomers. The home isn't yours, nor is the family. Instead, it might be the mother who lives up the street and takes in children to help offset any losses she might have sustained by not going back to work. This may be an ideal situation, since it's so close to home and you may know the parent. However, many such centers (estimates range as high as 90 percent) are not licensed, and, in fact, in thirty-two states, they need not be. In the states where licensing is required, the process may be perfunctory in the sense that the applicant does a self-inspection and fills out the papers.

As a matter of fact, many family day care facilities prefer not to be licensed. For example, there may be zoning regulations that they are violating. Going for a license means that they will be subject to all kinds of paperwork and that the monies they get are taxable. On the other hand, a licensed family day care center may be acceptable to welfare authorities, which means there will be state assistance available to offset the day care provider's costs.

Home Day Care Pluses And Minuses
The advantages:

1. You know the person and the house.

2. Her own children are in the house and you can tell a lot from them.

3. It's usually cheaper—a whole lot cheaper.

4. On occasion, the mother running the center will agree to keep a child overnight if there is an emergency.

Home Day Care Pluses And Minuses

The disadvantages:

1. A family day care is limited by law to taking six children including the owner's, only two of whom can be under the age of two. Not much socializing done that way.

2. Children living in the house can bully those who don't.

3. The day care owner may close down for her own family vacations and/or close in the summer.

4. Chances are she won't want her children exposed to your child's cold …but not vice versa.

5. And, if you get into a dispute with her, you can start a neighborhood feud.

You have another choice: You can quit your job and start your own family day care center. There are close to thirty sites that will tell you how (or sell you a starter kit) available through the Internet. These should give you an idea of what's involved in running your own family care facility.

The alternative to the "family care facility" is to turn to real, live, honest-to-goodness family members.

Relative Care

Care by relatives is common. In fact, grandparental care (by Granny-Nannies) is usually lumped into this category. But they are a separate animal and shall be dealt with separately.

In this case, when I say relative care, I don't mean boyfriends, and only reluctantly do I include uncles or brothers and cousins. Perhaps I have just read too many stories about males involved in shaken-baby cases. It may sound harsh to say this, but USE THEM AT YOUR OWN RISK.

Now, fathers are a different story. More and more fathers are staying home to raise their children. This most frequently happens when the mother has the better-paying job…or he hates his job and she loves hers…or at a time of widespread layoffs, he loses his job. If Father is available to care for the young ones, read no further.

But alas, Mr. Moms are few and far between, so most often one must look elsewhere in one's extended family for help.

This arrangement has its pluses—you can usually be fairly sure that your relatives have your child's best interests at heart, for instance. But there are minuses, too: if your relative also has a child, you can guess which one is going to come first in everything.

Relative care works best for people who have good relationships with relatives who, in turn, are flexible and are willing and able to help. If your sister reluctantly agrees to look after your baby, for example, it's probably best to pursue another option. You also have to be prepared to establish an employer–employee relationship with your relative, which can be tricky, especially if the relative is your elder. If the very thought makes you uncomfortable, then this arrangement may not work for you.

If you have a family member willing and able to take care of your child who shares your values and childrearing philosophy, consider yourself lucky. As long as you and your relative start out with a healthy relationship and are careful to maintain it, this inexpensive child care option is likely to provide your child with more love and security than any other solution. For example, as one mother said, "I care for my son (eighteen months) and my sister's children (thirty months and two months). I am glad for the opportunity for our children to grow up as close as siblings, and my sister and I have become the best of friends. We trust each other with our children and feel blessed not to have to send them to day care."

Relative care is the most inexpensive alternative to a Granny-Nanny. And if it takes place in the relative's home, it may be eligible for state child care subsidies and for child care deductions on your federal and/or state income tax return. Check it out.

Finally, there is . . .

CHAPTER 4

The Granny-Nanny

Lee Edwards Benning with her grandchildren Tara, Emma, and Paige.

Nobody can do for little children what grandparents do.
Grandparents sort of sprinkle stardust over
the lives of little children.

—Alex Haley

The simplest toy, one which even the youngest child can
operate, is called a grandparent.

—Sam Levenson

In the beginning there was the Granny-Nanny. In fact, there have always been Granny-Nannies. For millennia, in every civilization, in every tribe, she has been the matriarch who controlled every aspect of the upbringing of progeny, or the female unfit for manual labor who must justify her existence by minding the young ones, or the wise teacher who passed on the lore passed on by generations before.

The contemporary Granny-Nanny has changed a lot. Her hair rarely shows the slightest touch of gray. She wears pantsuits, with elastic waists and loosely fitted jackets, but when she wears a skirt, it's thinly pleated all around and is knee-length or longer. She's in much better shape physically because she's into walking, on a track or around the golf course or in the water for her arthritis. Hasn't worn a girdle in years, thanks to the genius who invented knee-highs and calf-length stockings. Her shoes are still sensible slip-ons or walking shoes, but she visits the podiatrist regularly. When it comes to Granny-Nannying, she knows about cross-cut nipples and the symptoms of earaches and allergies.

Whatever she looks like, she is still the Granny-Nanny whose kiss on a boo-boo works every time and to whom mothers naturally turn when day care is needed.

So, Who Is Minding The Children Now?

According to the Urban Institute's 1999 National Survey of America's Families (NSAF):

- 4 percent of children under the age of five are taken care of by nannies. However, according to the International Nanny Association, the number of nannies working in America grew by 25 percent between 1996 and 2001, and there still weren't enough to meet the demand for their services. In the case of severe shortages, one doesn't have much choice in the matter, and who knows whether the nanny you do find will be the right nanny for your child?

- 28 percent of children under age five are cared for in group day cares and preschools, and another 14 percent in family day care or a day care with between four and eight children: a total of 42 percent in all. Child care fields currently employ about 2.3 million workers, and opportunities in these fields are expected to grow at a faster than average rate through the year 2005 (U.S. Department of Labor, Women's Bureau). However—isn't there always a however?—there is the problem of finding the right one and then getting into it.

- 27 percent of children under age five are cared for by their parents.

- And the rest, the other 27 percent? The old-fashioned, traditional way, by relatives. In fact, 21 percent of all children under the age of five are cared for by their grandparents.

What is remarkable about the latter number is that it represents a nearly 50 percent increase from 1990 to 1997. How much higher will it go? With the loss and/or outsourcing of 66,000 jobs a month between 2000 and 2004, husbands and/or wives are being forced to take lower-paying jobs in the service industries, which means two have to work to bring home the same income as before. And in some families, the husband is holding down two jobs as well. So, many families can't afford day care and must turn to Granny-Nannies. For all of these reasons, experts believe that the number of grandparents providing child care may easily have doubled in the last five years.

What seems novel and even shocking to us is old potatoes to families in the United Kingdom and Australia, where, in fact, day care centers are NOT the first choice of parents—grandparents are! In fact, Aussie and Brit grandparents provide between 57 percent and 70 percent of all regular day care.

According to C. Everett Koop, M.D., Sc.D. and former Surgeon General, "nine out of ten grandparents will care for their grandchildren sometime this year." Some for short periods of time, some for longer ones, some on a regular basis, and some permanently. There are many sources of information for the latter— some of whom call themselves "second timers" or, more wryly, "second offenders"—but not much about those who share in the caring of a child.

Which is wrong. If available, grandparents should be the first choice of most parents. Why? In a word: trust. If the grandparents are your parents, you yourself are living proof of the excellence of their nurturing. If the grandparents are your spouse's, again you know firsthand the outcome of their nurturing since you married the result.

Further, you know that to a Granny-Nanny your child is not just another mouth to feed or diaper to change. That person's interest in your child is genuine, personal, and long-lasting. In a word, it's love. Love that can continue for decades, depending on the age of your Granny-Nanny. No other form of child care can offer you such assurance and insurance. Good old Granny-Nanny rides to the rescue of her children and her grandchildren . . . again.

That does not mean that all will be champagne and roses. There will be problems. Hopefully, not big ones or insurmountable ones. To forestall and/or solve those problems is one of the main purposes of this book.

PART II

And Whaddaya Think Of That?*

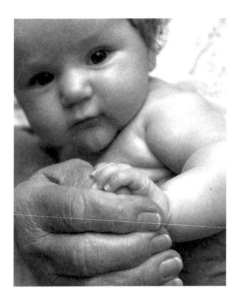

There are two sides
to every question—
a positive
and a negative one.

—Protagoras (485–421 BC)

But in the case of the Granny-Nanny, there are actually six sides to the question, since three parties have a vested interest in this situation. Whaddaya think of that? There is the parent's point of view, the grandparent's point of view, and, of equal or greater importance, the child's point of view. Each brings to the table a different set of criteria and a different concept as to what a Granny-Nanny is and isn't, should and should not be. In this modern version of Goldilocks, one wants too little, one wants too much, and one wants just the right amount. The question is: who wants what?

---

*With a hats-off to Laurie Berkner and her CD with the same title from Two Tomatoes Records. Haven't heard of Laurie yet? You will. She appears on the Noggin network and preschoolers love her. You will soon learn every single word of "We Are The Dinosaurs" and "Victor Vito," which will have your children singing of Tabasco and collard greens and other foods they won't be tasting for years.

CHAPTER 5

A Child's View
Of The Granny-Nanny

"I never thought Grammy and Gramps were babysitting.
I just thought we visited their house a lot."

"Nana is my best friend. So is Pop-pop."

So say two participants in different Granny-Nanny situations. The vast majority of such children agree.

Separation Anxiety

A child will accept nearly anything—including abuse (see Chapter 18, Abuse, page 138)—except for one thing: a mother's leaving—even temporarily. That is a major sin. A heart-breaker for the child each day . . . and for the Granny-Nanny who is an innocent victim of separation anxiety. She opens her heart and her arms to a grandchild only to be rejected, day after day after day. Of course, the rejection doesn't last forever, although it can go on for years or disappear only to return for a week or two. But it's wise to be prepared, to have a diversion, a distraction available: a problem to solve, something new to see, a treat to eat. Anything so long as the parent can make his or her escape. At which point, almost miraculously, tears dry up.

And if you think it only happens with young ones, you're wrong. Maybe there won't be the tears and pitiful cries, but one look at the desolation in their eyes . . . but enough of that.

What Children Want

What children want in a caregiver can be pretty well summed up in the word **nurture**. Yes, that means food and bed and clothes. But it means much more.

And the first of their many wants is the same regardless of age: they want to be loved, not just tolerated. For the younger ones, it's hands-on loving, hugs, kisses, physical demonstrations of love. Being swooped up and cuddled. Things their mother may not be able to do as frequently as she'd like to but a Granny-Nanny has all day to do.

For the older ones, a pat on the back or butt, a squeeze of the shoulder, even a quick nonembarrassing hug—boys like them, too, although they may not admit it.

Children want to be listened to. Really listened to. The worst thing a Granny-Nanny can do is to ignore them or put them off or talk over their heads. When one converses with children, look them in the eye, even get down to their level if your knees allow.

Children want adults to take pleasure in and enthuse about their accomplishments. They thrive on praise. Lots and lots of praise. There is more nourishment in a few words of praise than in a dozen bowls of Total cereal.

They need structure, too, which is frequently confused with discipline. Structure means a child's knowing his or her limits in terms of you and your environment. Where can they go . . . and not go? What furniture can they climb on . . . and not climb on (like glass tables, for example)? What cabinets can they open (very few) . . . and not open (most of them)? What doors can they open (most of them) . . . and not open (any doors to the exterior and any doors to bathrooms that are in use)?

Children do not particularly care whether your house is neat or not, but they sure like to have interesting things in it. A stack of graduated measuring cups is swell for young ones . . . washable crayons and black-and-white newspaper ads for older ones. Toys that just happen to be educational for the youngster. Games, which can be equally educational, for the older ones.

Did you know there are jigsaw puzzles for children as young as two? There is nothing like a jigsaw puzzle on a rainy day. Some people keep them set up almost permanently in a card table in the corner.

For a child, Granny-Nannying would be perfect if only the parents could stay home and share in it.

CHAPTER 6

A Grandparent's View Of
The Granny-Nanny

Becoming a grandmother is wonderful.
One moment you're just a mother. The next
you are all-wise and prehistoric.

—Pam Brown

Just about the time a woman thinks her work is done,
she becomes a grandmother.

—Edward H. Dreschnack

Most grandparents are very much aware of their own mortality. They are reminded of it by the obituary page in the daily newspapers and the obvious frailty of friends and contemporaries. Maybe that's why they realize so keenly their place in the family structure. Grandparents are both a connection to the past and a key to the future. They are the family's history, which in turn shapes the beings who continue to fill out the family tree. They set the values and standards by which families live, traditionally the same ones ingrained in them by their own grandparents and the generations who preceded them.

Sometime during the next year, up to 79 percent of grandparents will be called upon to provide some child care for their grandchildren. The number providing daily care nearly doubled between 1998 and 2003, according to the people at Childcare.org.

Of those caregivers, more than half are under age fifty-five. A third are between the ages of fifty-five and sixty-four. Fewer than one in five are over sixty-five. The vast majority are women.

Ronald Lee, a professor of demography at the University of California at Berkeley, has a theory that doting grandparents contribute to the longevity and long-term survival of the human race by nurturing not only their own offspring but grand-children as well. He found that in certain primates, the gender that provides the primary care to offspring tends to have a higher life expectancy, a fact that may explain why women live longer than men. Lee's "grandmother hypothesis" is that women experience menopause so they can become free from their own childbearing to care for grandchildren.

Most grandparents do not plan to take on such a full-time job, having already done their bit as parents. But they nonetheless take on the challenge and responsibility, often sacrificing their own physical, emotional, and financial health. Not to mention giving up a lot of their social life and retirement dreams. All that church work may have to go bye-bye. Same for doing much travel, taking up a new hobby (crocheting is back in, I'm told), gossiping with your neighbors, leisurely walks, or just plain relaxing with a good book or tear-jerking soap opera. As for those blessed afternoon naps? Gone. Unless your hearing is such that you can sleep with one ear open (more on that later).

Why do grandparents do it? Because they're needed—today's economic reality dictates that in most families both parents must work. Because grandparents love both their children and their children's children—they're flesh and blood. Because they want their grandchildren to get loving attention one-on-one instead of relegating those responsibilities to overworked, under-siege teachers and assistants in day care centers. Because, despite all the work and worry, it makes them feel good.

The Second Time Around

Not everyone gets a second chance to do it right, but Granny-Nannies do. Whatever niggling little things they didn't get right the first time around, they get the opportunity to do them right with the grandchildren. They can read them more and better books. They can take the time to help them learn their ABCs and how to count and how to name colors and how to say "thank you" and "you're welcome" and "pardon me" and "bless you" when someone sneezes. Table manners? Well, yes, persistence pays.

There's a bit of guilt involved for Granny-Nannies. They were younger and more self-centered when raising their own kids. They got all tangled up in the work process. And they wanted a life of their own beyond the forty- or fifty-hour workweek. So they tinkered around the house (or under the hood of the car), cut the grass, and tended the garden and washed their cars and tried to have some semblance of a social life, even if it meant taking along the kids.

Now that it's too late, maybe, just maybe, they think, they could have spent a few less hours at work and more hours playing with the children and teaching them life's fundamentals. Things the kids had to learn the hard way from someone else. Well, now grandparents have a chance to make amends. Now they can nourish a young body and mind and, at least on a part-time basis, help mold a perfect young lady or gentleman . . . sweet, polite, respectful, and appreciative.

It can be a gratifying experience. Preservation of family values and history is important to adults nearing the end of their lifespan. So is seeing the children reach goals as they grow: Halloween costume parades in preschool; dance recitals and scouting in grade school; academic achievements, athletic awards, school plays, and the like in their teens.

There's nothing more heartwarming than hearing a granddaughter say, "You're my favorite person, Nana," even though you may suspect she's using it to get something she wants. In many ways Granny-Nannying makes you feel young again (even though your aches and pains remind you that you're not). It puts some adventure back into what may have become a humdrum existence.

What's the downside to becoming a Granny-Nanny? From what I've read and heard and experienced, here are a few of the things you might expect:

- You're tired. You aren't used to keeping children's hours.

- Your arms ache from carrying even the smallest person.

- You say good-bye to your manicurist. Long nails and Granny-Nannying don't mix.

- You're frustrated by trying to keep so many balls up in the air.

- You feel guilt because you're not able physically to do the things with your grandchildren that you could do with your children.

- You regret the loss of hobbies and activities you once enjoyed but now have no time for.

- You have grown to hate the manufacturers of children's furniture, especially car seats (which may be why so many grandparents don't use them).

- Everything is too darn complicated, even infant swings.

- Everywhere you look there are straps to be fastened, even in grocery carts.

- The crying gets on your nerves.

- Your dog and cat have become jealous of the children because of lack of attention and they're "misbehaving," usually on the lightest-colored carpet in the house.

- You cringe at the thought of people dropping by since every toy in your house comes in a hundred pieces.

- You hate going back to everything-valuable-has-to-go-up-mantel-high-or-get-packed-away.

- You're tired of having every pillow on your bed thrown on the floor, buying tissues by the case, and having a potty insert drying in the sink.

And that's just for starters.

On the other hand, Granny-Nannying can turn couch potatoes into go-getters. All of a sudden grandparents are scouring garage sales for used toys, furniture, and playground equipment, a process that starts weeks or months before the first grandchild is born. They're buying CDs and cassettes and children's books for older ones. Getting reacquainted with *Little Red Riding Hood* and *Winnie-the-Pooh* and relearning the old standby nursery rhymes like "The Itsy Bitsy Spider" and "Baa Baa Black Sheep." Tirelessly pushing them on the swing and saying, "whee!" as they go down the slide. Clapping hands and saying, "well done" for every little accomplishment.

Does all of this joy and fulfillment have its drawbacks? You bet. It's hard work. A lot harder than it was the first time around. The back aches more. The knees creak like a rusty gate. The gumption just isn't as rampant anymore. It puts a strain on the retirement income. It takes a toll on the nervous system, not so much from worry, though that's part of it, but mostly from being just plain tired.

How do Granny-Nannies describe their experiences? Let me start with my own experience:

I'm proud to be a Granny-Nanny. I became one for a lot of good reasons, and with my eyes wide open (or so I thought). Ha! Hubris! I soon discovered that I—a mother, teacher, home economics graduate with a major in early childhood development, and author of a well-reviewed book on raising children on a budget—had little idea what I was up against.

Let me say up front that my daughter-in-law is as easy to get along with as you could ask for, and our granddaughters are angels—much easier to care for in many ways than was our son.

That said, there were problems: little, big, and many in between. Take, for example, my body ("Please!" as Henny Youngman would say). Despite years of activity, or maybe because of it, my lower back and knees protest the new demands being put upon them. The pain has me popping acetaminophen like crazy. And Pop-Pop, who is more than a bit older, is in just as bad shape. The upside is that lifting babies is as good as weight-lifting at the gym in terms of building upper-body strength.

Baby Bonus

On February 7, 2005, I underwent a total hip replacement. Two days later, in physical therapy, the therapist said, "You're stronger than women twenty years younger. Have you been doing strength-training?

I realized I had. For three years I had been lifting babies, starting with ten-pounders and graduating gradually to forty-pounders—forty pounds of wriggling, giggling grandchildren.

Within five days of surgery, I was walking without a cane—an unexpected bonus from Granny-Nannying.

More on health: I find that children's diets and geriatric diets don't always mesh. But worse, both my husband and I soon discovered that our resistance to childhood sicknesses had either gone AWOL or we were being besieged by mutant viruses that are much more formidable today than when we were young.

When the Chinese crud, the Florida flu, or the Colorado cough show up, they put us flat on our backs. There are times when a coffin seems better than all the coughin' . . . but I'm pleased to report that we survive the onslaught—eventually. The babies, meanwhile, are only mildly put out, and the parents generally don't feel a thing. Go figure. We've seen the internist more since we've started Granny-Nannying than we had in the previous decade—and flu shots, when you can get them, hurt like the devil.

Then there's our hearing. What did you say? Our hearing, as it is, isn't as good as it used to be. Despite that, most Granny-Nannies can hear a cry for help—"Nana, I'm stuck"—from a mile away and while soundly sleeping. They also can hear the cacophony when a child goes from one bleating toy to the next with no perceptible break in between. And once, way back, I had such a nice, quiet house and didn't go through life humming the original lyrics to the Barney songs.

Enough complaining. What about the upside? How can you put a price on the smile that lights her face in the morning when I say, "Hi, Paige"? Or the pride in helping Emma master "Look and Find" books while I sit on the toilet seat and she on the potty? Or the delight in having Tara use your forefinger as a teething ring? And hearing each successive grandchild learn to say "Nana" for the first time? Priceless. It's great being able to share a child's little triumphs. I feel very fortunate.

Was I normal in having mixed feelings of a) who needs this? and b) joy? I wasn't sure, so I reached out for help. Now where else would you expect a card-carrying member of the Doctor Spock–led generation to go but to books?

To my surprise, there were lots and lots of nanny books. Even one or two granny books dealing with what toys to buy and how to be a long-distance grandparent. Amazon.com says both types of books are big sellers, but the books didn't answer most of my questions. So I turned to my granny-aged friends and discovered that I wasn't the only one baffled by Granny-Nannying and struggling for helpful information.

I asked them a lot of questions, and they were enormously helpful. But I could tell that they were torn between a desire to help and worrying that they might be revealing family secrets. In some cases, I suspect, they may have been a little reluctant to discuss their own inadequacies in handling what we all agreed was a daunting task.

From it all—the books, the Internet, the gaggle of doting grandparents, and that best-of-all source of knowledge, the college of hard knocks—I have survived the first few years of Granny-Nannying in relatively good shape. The kids are developing just fine, thank you. Grandma and grandpa are older but wiser, and the communication with the parents is still first rate. What more can you ask?

So much for my own experiences. Here's what a select few of my Granny-Nanny friends had to say about theirs:

Granny-Nanny #1

"My daughter went back to work when her first daughter was ten weeks old. Lo and behold, Gramma became the full-time day care provider. Monday to Friday I was at my daughter's home from 7 A.M. to 2:30 P.M. Grandpa relieved me then because my full-time nursing job was from 3 to 11 P.M. Grandpa got relieved at 4 P.M. when my daughter arrived home.

"At six months I started taking the little one for swimming lessons at the Y, little knowing that they'd continue until she was five years old. For three years we went to the library hour every Tuesday. I watched her for eleven years and truly enjoyed every minute of it.

"When she was four, along came a little sister and the whole wonderful experience started all over again. This time I was an 'old pro'…older but wiser. We did many of the same things I'd done with my first grandchild, who was now in kindergarten and then school. Swimming, library, McDonald's. When she also went to school, I went through withdrawal.

"Would I do it again? In a second. Being a Granny-Nanny filled my life with so much love and fulfillment. It was a wonderful world filled with a whole bunch of warm fuzzies."

Granny-Nanny #2

"My grandchild's name is Kevin, but we call him Kebby. He is both a delight and a holy terror. We never know which we're going to get on a given day. So we just roll with the punches and do the best we can.

"Kebby means well, he's just full of it—and that's tough on a pair of sixty-six-year-olds. We're trying to get him ready for preschool, but as of now his behavioral problems would make it difficult. His parents and the doctor have considered putting him on a drug for ADD, but everyone is reluctant to rely on drugs if love and understanding will work.

"We'll just keep at it and hope that all turns out well. Meanwhile, both Mommy and Daddy have good jobs and are able to furnish their new house and provide a good home for Kebby and a little sister who is on the way. We've got our fingers crossed that she will be a little angel."

Granny-Nanny #3

"Being a Granny-Nanny is just about a full-time job for ten hours each weekday. We take care of a two-year-old granddaughter and a four-year-old grandson. We love them both, and I'm sure they love each other, but you'd never know it to watch them play.

"I guess play isn't the right word. What one has the other wants. What one wants to watch on TV the other doesn't like. Two TVs solve the problem for a few minutes. Two sets of toys helps, too. Other than that, we're about to resort to a referee's whistle.

"My advice to other Granny-Nannies is 'one is nice, but two may not be twice as nice.' I know that may be out of your control, and your kids may want lots of kids, so pray that they're all good-natured. It would also help if one of us hit the lottery. As tough as it is, we would do it again, as long as someone remembers that SR stands for senior and not sibling rivalry."

Granny-Nanny #4

"I wouldn't have believed it, but I absolutely love being a Granny-Nanny. I didn't know that's what it was called until I talked to you. It's a great name for it.

"I nanny three grandchildren, one, three, and four years. Two girls and the youngest, a boy. They call me Grammie and my husband Gramps. I couldn't do it without his help. Maybe one of these days he'll even learn how to change a diaper.

"What we like most about it is the joy of seeing them develop from helpless babies interested only in eating and sleeping to bright, active children eager to learn and eager to please. Maybe we're just lucky, but we're blessed with three well-behaved youngsters. Can't imagine how difficult it would be if they were little devils.

"Tell all those other Granny-Nannies out there that it's like the Frank Sinatra song, 'Love Is Better the Second Time Around.' Give 'em lots of love and they'll give it right back."

Granny-Nanny #5

"Thank God, it's over. My Granny-Nanny duty ended a few years ago, but I still remember how tough it was physically and emotionally. We took care of a girl and a boy who are now in third and fifth grade. They love school and are doing very well. Donna is taking ballet lessons and Josh is into Little League. I guess we did something right.

"It's a chore, but a worthwhile one. You get a lot of satisfaction not only while you're caring for them but also over the years as you see them turning into bright young kids. You just know they're going to be first-class citizens, and are proud that you played a big part in it. That's the really great part. But I'm still glad it's over and done with."

Granny-Nanny #6

"Do like Nike says, 'Just Do It!' Stop talking and start doing. Enough said."

CHAPTER 7

A Parent's View
Of The Granny-Nanny

You don't pay back your parents. You can't.

The debt you owe them gets collected by your children,

who hand it down in turn. It's sort of an entailment.

—Lois McMaster Bujold, *A Civil Campaign*

It is a fact of life: not all grandparents are the same. For example, there is:

The Granny-Nanny From Hell
(described by a young mother of four)

I wanted our kids to know one of their grandmothers, the way I knew my only one, so we hired her to watch our two kids (two and almost one) in our house while we both worked.

When things started to occur that bothered me, I was told to chalk it up to our getting used to each other. That was okay the first thirty days, but even though we told Grandma how we felt, she still did what she wanted to do, disregarded everything we said, and made me feel like she wanted to replace me in my own home. Among other things, just before taking her on as a sitter, we left her with the kids for two days for a mini-vacation. While we were gone, she rearranged our new house, every room right down to the pantry and refrigerator drawers; I spent the entire night putting everything back.

What else did she do? Here's a brief list:

- She insisted on changing the diet and nutrition habits of our kids in the interests of health, she said. My kids went from eating fruits and veggies to meat and potatoes … and some processed foods.

- She burned my expensive pot set and said nothing.

- She refused to brush our kids' teeth with toothpaste because on the back of the tube, it said do not use for kids under two unless you talk to your dentist. This we did. We talked to the dentist and the pediatrician and had their okay and yet she still didn't do it. But she pretended to do it.

- She refused to give amoxicillin to our son with an ear infection because she didn't like our pediatrician (she had never met him).

- She bought the kids clothes they didn't need at a thrift store, but I said nothing. Then she took all the clothes we had bought for them and shoved them in a drawer at the bottom of the dresser without telling us.

- She bought the kids toys at the thrift shop, no biggie, but it was stuff that shouldn't have been anywhere near the kids at their ages.

- But what really got me was the day our youngest apparently turned blue from something he put in his mouth. *She didn't call 911, she called her son.* By the time my husband came home, the child was fine. But by the time I got home, she had convinced my husband to get rid of many of the toys we bought and leave hers. My son never swallowed anything. I checked poop for days, and *wouldn't you call 911 if a kid in your care was turning blue?*

- She scared the pest control guy (who sprayed only the outside of the house for ants) so much that he refused to come again when she was there.

- She scared the grocery delivery guy, same result. No kidding. Neither said what exactly she did and neither knew the other, yet they had the same reaction.

- She opened my e-mails at home that should have gone to my work. So at work, I couldn't understand why I wasn't receiving notices until I got home. Then I saw them on the home computer. When she got caught at it, she told her son she thought that I could be cheating on him! Come on!! I was pregnant with our third kid, we had been married three years, I left for work half an hour before school started and was home directly after. . . . *continued on page 44*

Oh god, I am not kidding you on any of this, and writing this is a bit of a relief. While she raised her two sons right, the woman now has issues. After the opening of my work-related e-mails, I convinced my husband that his mother had to go. I had had it, and the stress wasn't good for me. I paid a friend an additional amount of money to take over for Grandma until the end of the year.

We now live in another state, and so does Grandma. I am pregnant with our fourth kid, and I am so glad she is six hundred miles away. My step-mom-in-law, she is awesome. I could have her around almost all the time.

Unbelievable? Not at all. Much of what the writer complains about will bring knowing nods from other mothers, even those in apparently successful Granny-Nanny situations.

The major source of problems between Granny-Nannies and parents can be summed up in that old adage, "Mother knows best." Which mother? The one who has already successfully raised children—"You kids weren't raised that way and you're healthy"—or the new, inexperienced mother who has done her research and is up on all the latest theories. You can think of it as Doctor Spock versus Doctor Brazelton, or even Doctor Phil.

And yet, even when a mother lists all her complaints—and they are considerable, and few mothers are reluctant to vocalize them—when the chips are down, parents still prefer grandparents over any other form of child care. Why? "Well, she's a pain in the arse at times, but I know she'd give her life for my kids."

Besides, she's cheap.

As for that grandmother from Hell? There are tens of thousands of other grand-parents, including mothers-in-law, about whom parents have nothing but praise.

Says one, "God, I must be an alien. I love my mother-in-law. She is a character." And another, "I get along better with my MIL [mother-in-law] than my mother." And a third, "Grandparents give the only love that money can't buy." And I could go on and on and on.

One mother, concerned about how good her son's grandmother was to him, said, "I'm afraid my child will think his grandmother is his mother."

Nope, wrong. This is one worry she needn't have. A child doesn't want another mommy, that position is already filled. (Which is why some stepparents have problems.) On the other hand, a child won't question his mother's decision as to who cares for him. She could put him in the hands of a sadist, an abuser, or worse, and he won't question it. As far as he's concerned, his mother can do no wrong. To a child, a parent is God—which is why so many children not only tolerate abuse but voluntarily return to it. It is shocking and sad, but it happens. And what a responsibility such innocence places on parents and Granny-Nannies alike.

However, greater than any concern thus mentioned is one single thought that all parents have: how safe will my child be? The safety of their children is their overarching concern, voiced over and over again in interview after interview. The only ones who worry more are the Granny-Nannies. Read on . . .

PART III

Child Safety

"It is the stuff of nightmares," said the parents of a toddler strangled by a window cord.

Between 1991 and 2004, the U.S. Consumer Product Safety Commission received 174 reports of child strangulation deaths that involved chains or cords on window coverings; 152 involved the outer pull cord while 22 were linked to the inner cord that runs through the window blind slats.

It is one of the worst of errors to suppose that there is any path for safety except that of duty.

—William Nevins

Nothing about Granny-Nannying, or parenting for that matter, is as nerve-wracking as the possibility that your charge will be injured or scarred, or hospitalized . . . or worse.

It would be easy to say don't sweat it, chances are slim to nothing, but that's not the answer. For one thing, it's not true. The chances of an accident happening are appallingly high. The concern is real. Yes, accidents happen, and yes, to one degree or another, they will happen to you. Your goal is to minimize their happening and know what to do when they do happen. You may think you know all there is about that sort of stuff, but you may be surprised at all that you have forgotten.

In which case a refresher course may be in order for all child care providers, especially when one realizes that, according to the National SAFE KIDS Campaign, **the number-one killer of children isn't disease, violence, or crime, but UNINTENTIONAL INJURY.**

With that in mind, this section will attempt to cover just about everything you need to know about child safety from boo-boos to broken bones . . . and then some.

Did You Know?

It's amazing what little hands can do and what little bodies can get into even in a cramped trailer or tiny apartment. Having a ranch house with basement just doubles the risk, and a two-story house with basement and attic quadruples it. All of which helps explain why it is imperative to make child safety a front-and-center issue. Just think of this:

- One hundred children in the U.S. die every day from avoidable accidents.

- Twenty-six million children are injured in or around the home each year.

- Two million children require medical attention each year from household accidents.

- Walkers for toddlers are responsible for 22,500 injuries per year.

- Two hundred children younger than age five die every year from choking on food, toys, or other objects.

- One million children accidentally ingest harmful medicines or chemicals each year, causing fifty deaths.

- Crib injuries account for more than forty deaths per year and 10,500 injuries, exclusive of SIDS (Sudden Infant Death Syndrome).

- Fifty thousand children are injured yearly playing with electrical cords, outlets, and appliances.

- Children start 100,000 fires each year, resulting in injuries and permanent crippling as well as deaths.

- Eighty-five percent of all U.S. homes built before 1978 contain lead-based paint, a critical hazard to children.

- More than 800,000 American children are reported as missing persons each year.

- Fifty percent of all crimes against children are committed by someone familiar to the child.

Scary, isn't it? I hope this hasn't so alarmed you that you have decided to forgo the love and gratification that comes from being a Granny-Nanny. But there is great truth, especially when it comes to children, in the saying that it is better to be safe than sorry.

Important Forms

Before you begin childproofing those homes, there's some paperwork to attend to. You'll need these forms in the event you need to seek medical help for the children. Note, each of the two forms that follow should be filled out for each child. The Emergency Information Form will provide a capsule medical history of the child, which a doctor and/or emergency room may need. And the Emergency Permission Form gives the Granny-Nanny permission to agree to treatment. It, too, should be filled out, signed, and notarized for each child. I suggest the latter be dated on each child's birthday, which will make updating easier. Similar forms are available, by the gross, over the Internet.

Emergency Information Form

Child's Name: _____

Date of Birth: _____

Social Security Number: _____

Medical Insurance Company: _____

Policy Number: _____

Parent/Guardian's Name: _____

Home Address: _____

City, State, Zip: _____

Home Telephone: _____

Mother's Work Number: _____

Father's Work Number: _____

Cell Phone Number(s): _____

Pediatrician or Family Physician: _____

Physician Telephone Number: _____

Dentist: _____

Dentist Telephone Number: _____

Known Allergies: _____

Known Illnesses: _____

Date of Last: Tetanus Shot _____ Mumps _____

Measles _____ Rubella _____ DPI _____ MMR _____

Medications taken regularly: _____

Emergency Permission Form

I, _____ (Parent/Legal Guardian),

hereby authorize emergency medical treatment for:

_____

in the event of an emergency accident, illness, or injury. I understand that this authorization does not cover emergency major surgery unless:

a) All attempts to contact the parent or legal guardian prior to surgery are unsuccessful, and

b) The medical opinions of two licensed physicians, concurring in the necessity for such surgery, are obtained prior to the performance of any surgery.

_____

Signature of Parent/Guardian

Date_____

Witness_____

CHAPTER 8

Childproofing Your Home

I childproofed everything in the house by the book . . .

and yet my kids seem to have figured out all the gadgets.

Things aren't childproof, they're parentproof!

—A mother in Colorado

Where to begin? Some people start with the cheapest make-do's that they can. Others say, "hang the expense," and go for the most dangerous rooms in the place. The good news is that most changes aren't all that expensive. (I'm not talking cribs and things, which we'll get into later—see Money Matters, page 99.) These are the "must-do's" in making the child's environment as secure as possible, whether it is Granny-Nanny's home or the parents', a house or an apartment:

• **Place all pill, liquid, and paste medicines out of reach,** remembering that the child's reach increases with every passing day. Be especially careful with aspirin and iron supplements, the number-one and number-two poisoning products. Be sure to switch prescription medications back to childproof lids (although, in my opinion, they are a joke. Many an arthritic grandparent can't open them, so her grandchildren do it for her).

• **Secure all household cleaning and pest control products** from curious, investigating little hands and mouths. If you can't find a place for them other than under the sink, find a way to fasten those doors so that only adults can open them.

• **Find secure places for makeup, vitamins, haircare products, suntan lotions, mouthwash, soaps, bleach, insect sprays, and just about anything else made by a chemical manufacturer.**

• **Cover all electrical outlets.** Safety plugs are readily available. While you are at it, try to make sure cords that must be utilized, such as those on lamps and appliances, are not easily pulled from outlets. Bending the prongs may help.

• **Lock or otherwise fasten cabinet doors and drawers.** Inquisitive little minds love to see what's behind or within, and constantly having to say "no" will only increase your frustration. A tip: Facing cabinet doors can be fastened by placing strong rubber bands around the two knobs. Alas, that may only work until the babes are old enough to figure out the subterfuge. On the other hand, our toddler granddaughters have been known to carefully replace accidentally unfastened rubber bands. One never knows.

• **Check all furniture for tip-over** and don't mistake a well-known name brand for a guarantee of safety. We purchased a gliding rocker that tipped the first time I leaned over to pick up a bottle because the rockers were not spaced far enough apart. That episode ended with the Product Safety Commission (and yes, please report such incidents and protect other young ones) chasing down all such models.

• **Be especially wary of footstools and stepstools** since children love to climb. Check the legs. They should extend out far enough at the bottom that there is a straight line from the edge of the seat to the foot of the leg. Those with nicely, decoratively tucked-under legs are also nicely, decoratively tippable. As a rule of thumb the piece should be as deep as it is high. Think of a square as being harder to tip over than a rectangle.

• **If an object is tipsy or rickety or antiquey, think about putting it away** until the kids are big enough to know better and are able to reason clearly. Don't ask when that will be, no one knows. For some children it will be by the time they go to kindergarten, for others it's when they're off to college.

• **Hike up out of reach dangling cords on blinds, curtains, lamps, etc.** They are irresistible to young hands. Lamp cords are difficult, but with a little ingenuity you can tape or tie them to table legs or hide them in places children can't access.

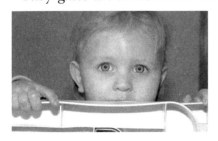

• **Baby gates are an absolute necessity at the top of any stairs,** even those two- or three-step ones. But to be safest, don't rely on a pressure gate. Take the time and trouble to install gates with screws or lag bolts and make sure the fastening device is also secure. Put the gates either at the top or the bottom of the stairs, depending on where the child will spend time. If there is going to be much up and downing of the stairs, as in a split-level house, consider putting gates at both the top and the bottom of each run of steps.

• **Remove all small rugs** and anything that can be tripped over by tiny feet. What to you looks like a tiny change in elevation can be a small mountain to a child.

• **Put your household plants out of reach.** Dirt has a magical way of winding up in little hands and thence onto your carpets and hardwood floors, not to mention the generous amount that finds its way to the mouth. And if the plant sits in a watering pan, realize that water is a powerful attractant as well. Mix the two together and you have early mudpies. Ugh! However, I am assured by several grandchildren that they are delicious.

• **Pick up all small objects from the floors of the rooms to which the infants will have access.** Not just because you don't want them swallowed (anything up to one and a half inches in diameter is fair game), but also because otherwise you'll be picking them up several times a day. Best advice: put them up high or store them away until your Granny-Nannying days are over.

• **Trade in those lever-type doorknobs for regular round ones.** Your little charges can easily pull down a lever—one of ours could do it at twenty months, but she was four before she could manage to twist a round knob.

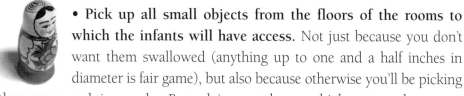

• **Make sure all exterior doors can be locked from within**—and not unlocked by little hands.

• Another outside door protection: **hang a strip of jingle bells or a cowbell on the door** to alert you when the door opens. Stores have them, why not homes?

• **Fasten crib toys on the wall side only** so the infant can't use them to climb up and fall.

• **Keep furniture away from windows** so children can't crawl up and fall out. Window glass is a hazard, and never trust a screen to prevent a fall.

• **A display case with glass doors can be dangerous** if a child falls against the glass. If you think you have one that's a hazard, place an "X" of clear two-inch tape over the glass as a temporary safety measure. (Blue painter's tape is more unsightly but more protective.) It goes without saying that you should either fasten the doors or move your collectibles to higher shelves.

• **Keep matches and lighters in high-up safe places.** Fires kill more people each year than floods, hurricanes, tornadoes, and earthquakes combined.

• **Check your home for old paint, which may contain lead.** Kids have a way of gnawing on window sills and the legs of hand-me-down furniture, as well as the rails of older painted playpens and cribs. Elevated levels of lead in the blood can cause brain damage and learning and behavioral problems. Suggestion: don't just paint over old, disintegrating paint; scrape or strip and sand before repainting. Always wear a mask when dealing with old paint.

• **Turn your water heater down to 120 degrees or lower.** A child's skin can be burned in seconds by water above that temperature. Don't know how to do it? Call your plumber or furnace man and get instructions over the phone.

• If you feel the need, **don't hesitate to employ the services of a professional child safety expert.** These experts get down on their knees to view dangers unseen by grandparents with aching backs and crickety joints. You can choose to merely get recommendations from the safety expert, or he or she will make the changes if you so desire. In either case, the expert will be a valuable source of knowledge and a resource for getting the finest safety products. To find a safety-proofer, contact the International Association of Child Safety at 1-888-677-IACS. They are a nonprofit organization, and their services are free. Not so those of the child safety expert they may recommend.

Apartment Building Safety

Elevator Safety

The thing about apartments is that everything is on one level (except for you lucky duplex-dwellers), which is good for aged knees and for keeping track of kids. On the other hand, everything is probably not at street level, which is bad —unless you are in an elevator building.

Some buildings have elevator operators, who are under orders never to allow children to help them work the machinery. However, in the interests of keeping down costs, many elevated buildings have switched to automatic elevators with push buttons for each floor. Children who can count and recognize numbers may be permitted by Granny-Nanny to push the correct button, always assuming the child can reach high enough and Granny-Nanny is standing close by.

For younger children, make a point of always keeping your body between the controls and the child while pushing "open door" or "close door" buttons. An exception: the red alarm button, which all children should learn to use if necessary. Try to keep your apartment door dead-bolted when the children are there so they can't access the elevator, especially if the elevator's panic button is actually a telephone set up so high that children cannot reach it.

I should point out that certain Granny-Nannies have confessed they can keep a child amused by the hour by letting them play elevator operator. Fellow tenants and landlords may not appreciate it. I'd double-check that children can't access either the roof or the basement—both danger zones.

Around and About

With an infant, you'll need a stroller. Make sure it folds and unfolds easily, preferably with one hand, because you'll be taking it everywhere—out on the street, on buses, down the subway stairs, onto the train, up the stairs, and back out on the street. The stroller should have lots of storage in it because from now on, until the child can walk, it's going to double as your grocery cart. After that, your grocery cart will serve as a stroller.

Stairs—horrible things, but better than ladders. Turn your trips into lessons in counting (which gives you an excuse to stop now and then to catch your breath).

If you can't handle children and carry groceries, find a store or a supermarket that delivers. There are more and more of them around.

Toilets. Children love to flush things. In a house, it's a matter of calling the plumber; in an apartment building, you may need to summon the landlord or super. There are devices that can be fastened to toilet lids to make them close automatically. Invest in one.

Noise. Nothing you can do about it, children are noisy, and many apartment buildings have rules about carpeted floors for a quieter existence. You can abate children's noise by keeping them in sneakers or slipper-socks instead of hard-soled shoes. Nothing wrong with bare feet either. If possible, choose a child's play area in that part of the apartment farthest from your grouchiest neighbor. Keep TV sets and the like turned down low. Children as a rule have much, much better hearing than you do . . . and you really don't need to hear much of children's programming. It is a wise idea, however, to keep the remote up high lest channel-surfing be ongoing. (If you have a cable company that has a parental "lock" to deny access to certain channels, make use of it.)

Commonsense Child Safety Rules

Having childproofed your home, you need to set some rules for yourself and your spouse or anyone else who helps you care for your grandchildren.

Nap Time

Young children up to the age of thirty months may take two naps a day, and some will give up the morning nap at around twenty-four months. Those up to the age of five may still take an afternoon nap. Remember, each child is an individual and sleeping needs will differ. Try to establish consistent nap times with the child's parents so the child goes down at the same time wherever he is. That will lessen the fussing and the arguing.

Stay within hearing distance while the infant is sleeping. You'll want to check out strange noises, coughs, sneezes, choking sounds, cries, whimpers, and who knows what else. If the infant's bedroom is a distance away, invest in a monitor and turn up the volume. Remember that your hearing may not be as sharp as it was a few decades ago, so play it safe.

The nice thing about nap time is that it's like recess for you. You can use the time to do a favorite thing, which shouldn't include taking a nap yourself unless you have exceptionally good hearing or a monitor right next to your head. Read a good book. Listen to music. Relax your mind and body. Soon enough nap time will morph into change-my-diaper time.

Cribs

According to the federal government, four million babies are born each year, but only one million new cribs are sold. Which ipso facto leads us to the conclusion that there are a lot of secondhand or hand-me-down cribs in use each year. That's fine and makes sense, providing the cribs are safe.

If you are Granny-Nannying an infant in your own home instead of the parents' home, be sure the crib you have meets current child safety standards:

- The main criterion is that **the maximum distance between the slats should be no more than two and three-eighths inches. New cribs will qualify. Anything older than 1986 won't.** (So that beloved antique crib up in the attic? Forget it unless you put mesh around the interior.) Buying a used crib? Use a ruler or try to insert a soda can between the slats. If the can slides through, the crib won't do.

- **Watch out for fancy cut-outs in the head or foot** in which an arm or foot can be stuck.

- **Crib posts in the corners can be dangerous if high enough for clothing to get stuck on them,** which could result in your grandchild's strangling.

- **Beware of painted cribs—lead-based paint may have been used.** Today's painted cribs come with plastic covers for the sides to prevent teething infants from devouring the crib. To be safe, **do not buy a crib with chipped paint.**

- Needless to say, make sure there are **no loose hardware parts**.

- Be certain that **the crib itself is sturdy enough to withstand a whole bunch of kangaroo jumps**.

- One more thing: **I make it a rule to never, ever put a side down**. If children don't know it can happen, they may never try it. In case they do, **be sure the latch is not a simple pressure lever.**

- **The mattress should be firm and flat and brand-new for hygiene reasons.** The important thing is not the number of coils or whatever, but that it **fit the crib tightly.** So tightly that a child's foot cannot get between the crib and the side. We're talking two or fewer of your fingers here passing between mattress and crib. It will make putting fitted sheets on it a hassle, but the infant won't be able to get himself wedged between mattress and crib.

- **Bumpers are fine if securely fastened at all corners and at least once on each side.** They help protect the baby that insists on sleeping as in the womb, with his head against something firm. And they prevent drafts. Where they become dangerous is when the child begins to stand. Then they make a perfect step up and over the crib side.

Always place the infant on its back, contrary to the now-debunked myth that the child is better off on its tummy. That's what the latest Sudden Infant Death Syndrome safety guidelines state.

You'll find that there are myriad crib toys out there that dangle from above or attach to the rails. And as many as you'll find at a chain store you'll also find at garage and yard sales for pennies on the dollar. Try to determine which ones are least likely to present a safety problem. For example, mobiles with hanging toys should have strings no longer than seven inches.

When Too Much Of A Good Thing Is A Bad Thing!

Grandparents belong to the can't-have-too-much-of-anything school of thought. When it comes to crib toys, that's a no-no. Don't load up every possible inch of that space and create visual overload for the kid. If you purchase more than two or three such toys, put some aside and rotate their use every few weeks. Surprisingly enough, as compared to us easily bored old-timers, children do not get tired of toys. They may outgrow them, but they don't get bored with them.

Music can be soothing and sleep-inducing. The tunes produced by musical toys are better than nothing but will get on your nerves after the gazillionth playing. Better to play a nice CD or the Soundscapes channel on your TV. My own preference is the Light Classical channel. It soothes my Granny-Nanny nerves, and who knows what good might come to the child from a steady dose of classical music while growing up?

Crib Safety Resources

To be doubly safe, check with the Consumer Product Safety Commission (www.cpsc.gov/) for recent recalls of cribs, etc. For example, back in 2000, the CPSC warned about the safety of cribs being used in hotel rooms. If you're going on a trip and ordering a crib for the room, ask if the crib meets current standards.

Play Time

Toys are for fun. Toys are for education. Toys are not supposed to injure. Yet in 2002 more than 212,000 children went to the hospital emergency room for toy-related injuries—and of those children, thirteen died.

We know so much about toy injuries because in 1958 a National Clearinghouse for Toy Injuries was created. Then in 1973, Congress created the CPSC, which closely monitors and regulates toys. It has the authority to develop and enforce safety regulations for consumer products and spends more than half its budget on children's items alone. Any toys that have been made in—or imported into —the United States after 1995 must comply with the CPSC's Child Safety Protection Act. This includes toy standards for things like the paint used on toy surfaces, noise levels, sharp edges, small parts, and flammability.

According to ChildProductSafety.com, a service of the Arkansas attorney general's office, more than seven hundred toys and children's products have been recalled since 1986. They include animals, stuffed and not stuffed, balls—can you think of anything less harmful than a ball? Maybe a book? There was a recall of one of those in 2004. To continue: bathtub toys; blocks and sorting toys; boats; books; buses; cars; chests; clowns; dolls; games; guns (personally, I'd ban the lot of them); helicopters; holiday and seasonal items (wouldn't it make your holiday splendid if Santa delivered a knock-out, or should I say choke-out, toy?); cribs and strollers (which I personally do not consider toys); jewelry (jewelry for kids? no way!); musical instruments; planes; play sets and activity sets; playhouses; puppets; puzzles; ride-on toys; sports toys; telephones; trains; trucks; and whistles. Whew! Try to keep these in mind when you go to the next garage sale.

Yes, toy companies test toys for safety. They do so by consulting child development experts. More important, they test the toys on infants and preschoolers during supervised play at lab facilities. A toy may go through more than one hundred tests in the attempt to duplicate the wear and tear on and use of a toy by an active child. Yet still, despite this, Associated Electrics, Inc., Aviva, Graco, Hasbro, Lakeshore Learning, Mattel, and others recalled toys in 2004. As did Kmart, Target, Babies "R" Us, and FAO Schwarz.

Toy Safety Resources

If you'd like to check to see whether a toy has been recalled, go to the CPSC's website and click on Recalls and Product Safety News at www.cpsc.gov.

A little easier to use because it is divided into categories is the recently mentioned website of the Arkansas attorney general, www.childproductsafety.com.

By the way, the age level listed on a toy doesn't mean it's right for that age group, just that it should be safe for that age range.

To get the right age-appropriate toys, check out Appendix 4 (page 209), with suggestions for toys for all ages from the American Academy of Pediatrics.

Indoor Play Time

Okay, so you have a few "age-appropriate" toys, meaning they shouldn't do dire harm to your grandchild. What next? Things will go a lot easier for you if you can confine toy use to one room or area. For obvious reasons, all or most of the flooring in the play area should be cushioned by carpets. It takes a bunch of falls before the crawler becomes a toddler. And a whole bunch more before the toddler becomes a Junior Olympian.

Resign yourself to picking up toys. It's part of the routine. But keep the number of toys to a minimum; wall-to-wall toys make it difficult to crawl and walk. A sizable toy chest is recommended, preferably one with a stop-hinged cover that won't automatically slam on little fingers. Keep the toy chest filled. Half of the fun for the little ones is pulling out the toys. The tricky part is getting them to put them back.

Watch out for that walker. Unless they have mobility disabilities, infants and toddlers should not be put in walkers. Way too many accidents stem from too-early walker use. Some experts say walkers also hinder walking development. A stationary Exersaucer is okay, if you supervise and don't just treat it as a babysitter.

Playing Outdoors

When younger children play outdoors, whether in a yard, a beach, a public park, or a playground, make sure the area has a protective surface such as sand, wood chips, recycled and shredded tires, or some other commercially available playground material that will cushion falls.

Use your common sense about the size of such equipment as slides, swings, monkey bars, and bouncing animals. The younger the child, the smaller the equipment should be. For the very young, there are now excellent swing seats that fully enclose the child. And plastic slides come in enough heights and levels of complexity to suit any age. (And they have been known to come into the house during winter so rambunctious children could go "whee" when the weather was bad outside.)

Supervised play is a big key. You need to be there to kiss a boo-boo or push a swing or hold a hand while your grandchild goes "whee" down the slide. Put a bench or lawn chair in close proximity. You'll need a rest long before the tot is tired. Take your cell or a cordless phone with you so you don't have to leave the child unattended while you take a call.

For a play area in your yard, if possible enclose the area to counteract wanderlust. It will keep the child from getting out onto the street and also keep away stray dogs. If you have a dog of your own, the fence will keep the play area free of doggie doo-doo. If the child is playing in a public park or playground, bring along some baggies so you can do the ground-keeping that pet owners should have done.

In general, let the child tell you when the time is right to use a certain toy. You may want to show off how soon your charge can operate a beep-beep car, but forcing the child into new and challenging situations too soon can harm his or her development. Be patient. Let children find their own way. After all, you want to raise a superhero, not a scaredycat.

For information about accidents and dangers connected with outdoor play equipment, consult the report by the Consumer Product Safety Commission: www.cpsc.gov.

Chow Time

No adult eating implements for the first three years, please. Long handles and sharp points are a no-no. Little eyes are precious. There are lots of safe plastic spoons with easy-grip handles on the market.

Food choices should be dictated by the parents. Don't try new foods without checking with them first.

Allergies

Here is where your experience may really come in handy. If you are familiar with allergic reactions in young babies and you see something similar in your grandchild, speak out! And loudly. If the pediatrician pooh-poohs the idea, accompany the grandchild and his mother on the next visit to the doctor. There is something intimidating about an aroused grandmother who probably has several decades on the doctor.

It is your responsibility to watch for signs of allergic reactions to foods and beverages. Just because you loved peanut butter sandwiches when you were young doesn't mean your grandchild won't be allergic to peanuts … or for that matter to wheat, whole milk, strawberries, spinach, eggs, and a host of other substances.

Use a safe high chair with a tray that clicks into place securely and a seat belt strong enough to withstand the most violent lunges. It should go without saying that the high chair legs should be properly spaced to prevent tipping.

Diaper-Changing Time

It's a dirty job, but someone has to do it. When it's just you and the child, wherever you are, you're elected.

For your own home, if you don't want to splurge on an all-out baby-changing station like Mommy's, invest in a table-top changing unit with a safety strap. Place it on a sturdy cabinet or table, preferably near the crib, parallel to and against a wall. That way you block the child with your body and prevent him from rolling over toward you. Use the safety straps . . . always. It's a good habit to cultivate. Keep one hand on the child . . . always. It's another good habit to cultivate.

Keep the diapers handy so that you don't have to leave the child to go get them. Use a Diaper Genie if you and/or your arthritic hand can conquer it. Otherwise, a diaper pail with a lid and a foot pedal should be at hand, again so you never have to leave the baby's side during changing. The baby powder and any lotions or creams should be handy, but out of the reach of grasping hands.

Bath Time

Leave the bathing to Mom if you're just day-sitting. That is unless you encounter a mudpie massage or a peanut-butter-and-jelly belly. If you're doing overnight duty, or Mom and Dad are taking a long weekend, you'll probably want to do the bath thing. And here's what you need to think about.

For an infant, use a suitably sized tub placed high enough so you won't get a crick in your back. But make sure it is settled securely on a solid surface. The drain-board of your kitchen sink is perfect. Be sure that the tub is not so deep or so full of water that it increases the danger of drowning. **Remember, an infant can drown in one inch of water.**

Testing the water temperature with your elbow may have worked when you were younger, but no longer. Use your wrist instead. If it feels hot to you it will feel hotter to the infant, whose skin is thinner and more sensitive. Hopefully, you will already have set the water heater control to 120 degrees or less. Anything above that can burn tender skin.

Never, ever leave a child unattended in the tub for even a minute. It's just too dangerous at any age up to four or five.

Bath toys are fine so long as they are too large to be swallowed, too soft to cut or bruise, and too cute to ignore. Nemo is right at home in the tub.

Christmas Joy ... Or Horror

Christmas is a special time of year for families, and especially for children and their caregivers. It is also the time of year, every year, when about 12,500 people go to the emergency room because of holiday-related injuries, according to the U.S. Consumer Product Safety Commission. Additionally, Christmas trees are the cause of between 300 and 400 fires a year, resulting in as many as 150 deaths, 1,200 injuries, and between $10 million and $15 million in property loss and damage.

Tree Safety — Live Christmas Trees

The National Christmas Tree Association says up to 40 million families in the United States will purchase live trees this year. Another 7.3 million will purchase an artificial tree.

Keep these facts in mind when buying a live tree to make sure you're not buying a potential fire hazard:

- The tree should be green.

- It should be difficult to pull the needles from the branches.

- The needles shouldn't break when bent between your fingers.

- The trunk butt should be sticky with resin.

- When the trunk is bounced on the ground, needles shouldn't shower to the ground.

When you get the tree home, put it as far away from the fireplace as is consistent with the Santa story. If you buy an artificial tree, make sure it is fire-resistant.

As For Decorations,

- Use noncombustible or flame-resistant materials.

- Never use lighted candles on a tree.

- If you have small children, refrain from using decorations that are sharp or breakable.

Lights Are The Real Danger.

- Only use lights that have been tested for safety (look for a designated label on packaging).

- Discard any damaged sets.

- Never use electric lights on a metallic tree.

- Turn off all lights when you go to bed or leave the house.

- **Use no more than three standard-size sets of lights per extension cord**—this is the most frequently unobserved rule.

More Tips For A Safe And Healthy Christmas

Child safety expert Martin Simenc, president of Home Safety Services in Redwood City, California, and a member of the International Association for Child Safety, offers these tips:

- Watch where you leave bowls of tiny pinecones or potpourri, wreaths, ornaments, nativity scenes, and any other decorations with unsecured pieces that can choke children. Keep candy-filled dishes on high tables or counters. Clean up carefully when wrapping presents, because kids will be attracted to scraps.

- Strings of electric lights are dangerous because children can get wrapped up in the wires and risk strangulation or even electrocution. Tinsel is just as irresistible and dangerous. If you use strings of lights of any kind, hang them high and keep your children away from the outlets.

- If your tree isn't anchored securely to its stand, your child may reach for a low-hanging bough and pull the whole thing down. Be sure decorative items cannot be toppled by giving them a good "shake test."

- Consider setting up your tree and other decorations outside the primary play area and putting up a safety gate to block your child from entering the room.

- Although poinsettias are not poisonous to humans, consuming large amounts can cause cramping and diarrhea. Mistletoe, when ingested, will cause severe stomach cramps and diarrhea and can even be fatal. If you decide to hang some over your doorway, make sure it's well secured and won't be knocked to the floor where pets and young children could happen upon it. Holly and Pyracantha are toxic as well. If you suspect poisoning from any plant source, contact your local poison control center immediately.

The Laws Of A Toddler

Toddlers think differently than we do. And you've got to know their rules. Among the many reasons for going to these great lengths to childproof your home, consider what might happen when the laws of a toddler prevail.

TODDLER RULES

If it is a potty, it is to be played with, not peed in.

If it is on, I must turn it off.

If it is off, I must turn it on.

If it is a liquid, it must be shaken, then spilled.

If it is a solid, it must be crumbled, chewed, or smeared.

If it is high, it must be reached.

If it is shelved, it must be removed.

If it is pointed, it must be run with at top speed.

If it has leaves, they must be picked.

If it is plugged, it must be unplugged.

If it is not trash, it must be thrown away.

If it is in the trash, it must be removed, inspected,
and thrown on the floor.

If it is closed, it must be opened.

If it does not open, it must be screamed at.

If it has drawers, they must be rifled.

If it is a crayon, it must write on the refrigerator, monitor, or table.

If it is full, it will be more interesting emptied.

If it is empty, it will be more interesting full.

If it is a pile of dirt, it must be played in.

If it is a stroller, it must under no circumstances be ridden in without protest. It must be pushed by me instead.

If it has a flat surface, it must be banged upon.

If Mommy's hands are full, I must be carried.

If Mommy is in a hurry and wants to carry me, I must walk alone.

If it is paper, it must be torn.

If it has buttons, they must be pressed.

If the volume is low, it must go high.

If it is toilet paper, it must be unrolled on the floor.

If it is a drawer, it must be pulled upon.

If it is a toothbrush, it must not be inserted into my mouth.

If it has a faucet, it must be turned on at full force.

If it is a phone, I must talk to it.

If it is a bug, it must be swallowed.

If it doesn't stay on my spoon, it must be thrown to the floor.

If it is not food, it must be tasted.

If it IS food, it must not be tasted.

If it is dry, it must be made wet with drool, milk, or toilet water.

If it is folded, I must unfold it.

If it is Mommy, it must be hugged.

CHAPTER 9

On The Move

In America there are two classes of travel—first class,
and with children.

—Robert Benchley

The best car safety device is a rearview mirror
with a cop in it.

—Dudley Moore

There is travel, and then there is travel! Long distance, medium, and short. Airplane, train, bus, car, bicycle—if it moves, you may find yourself coping with it.

Whichever way you go, for anything but a trip around the block—stop right there, even a trip around the block via stroller means some packing up needs to be done in a formal diaper bag or improvised plastic bag or handy backpack, or if you're lucky, a pocket. The contents? Diapers, wipes (nobody uses talcum these days), plastic bags for disposal, age-appropriate food, toys (nothing valuable, please, they're apt to go astray, and you'll have neither time nor inclination to chase after them), weather-wear, and, of course, that particular "precious" no young child can leave at home.

Once packed, you're off! On an adventure. A nice one, hopefully, sans crying and the like.

Going By Airplane

You bring your own car seat for any child over the age of two (and pay the fare). A child under the age of two flies free, but in your lap. Some airlines have souvenirs for children, coloring books, and similar items—but don't count on it. Bring things for the child to do. Ditto for meals and snacks. Stewards usually will warm bottles. Some restrooms have teensy-weensy areas for diaper changing. Other than that, the main disadvantage to traveling with a nannikin is that the changes in air pressure can cause earaches, and some children will howl throughout the trip as other passengers scowl. Oh, but you do get to get on the plane first.

Going By Train

Still one of the safest modes of transportation available despite stories you may have read about derailments. Robert Buck, Director of Transportation for the Southeastern Pennsylvania Transportation Authority, suggests the following:

• **Stand back from the edge of the platform.** If the platform is crowded, stand even farther back. Don't worry that you won't find a seat, you can usually count on the conductor to help you find one. **HOLD ON TO THE CHILD'S HAND**… and use a death grip.

• **Boarding the train** can be difficult. (Personally, I think the designer of train steps was a giant.) The child should precede you so you can help lift if necessary. Don't worry about the train taking off without you. The conductor, who is on the train platform, has to signal an all-clear before the train can leave.

• **Moving between passenger cars** involves opening and closing heavy doors. **Avoid if possible.**

• **Stay seated until the train comes to a complete halt.** Let other passengers get off first to avoid bumping and jostling. The adult should exit first and the child second.

• **Before boarding or after disembarking, beware of the train crossings.** Even though there are whistles and guardrails, don't rely on them. Make sure to look both ways before crossing any track . . . and never, but never cross except in designated crossing places.

Going By Subway Or Elevated Train

Again, very, very safe provided you exercise common sense.

• **Hold the child's hand.** If the child is small, use a three-finger grip on the hand and wrap your ring finger and little finger around the child's wrist. With a very small child, hold her in your arms.

• **Stand back from the edge of the platform.** If the platform is crowded and there is some chance of being jostled, stand even farther back. You may end up being the last one to board the train, but that's the price you pay for safety.

Although courtesy is on its last legs, a direct request of a single person occupying a double seat often results in the seat being relinquished to you. Try to time your outing so that you are not competing with commuters for space and seats.

• Again, **the child should enter the subway first** with you giving assistance . . . and the opposite when exiting.

• **Remain seated** until the subway comes to a complete halt. Many accidents happen from overeager passengers losing their balance while rushing for the doors before the train has completely stopped.

Going By Bus

Actually, we're talking two kinds of buses here, the public transit type and the school bus. Many children will go through their entire lives without traveling on a city bus, but rare is the child who doesn't find himself riding a yellow bus.

Public Bus Travel

Robert Buck offers the following advice for public transit riders:

• **Stay back from the curb.**

• **Hold the child's hand.**

• **Let the child enter the bus first.**

• **Sit behind the driver if possible** (these seats are usually reserved for the elderly and/or handicapped; a Granny-Nanny qualifies).

• **Steady the child with your hand.**

• **Exit the bus from the front—the adult descending first.** This has several advantages. First, on some buses, the driver can lower the step so it will be easier for a small or older person to exit. Second, the driver can see the child descend from the bus, which may not be possible from side or rear exits.

By Preschool Bus

My own thoughts about nursery school busing are that even if my nursery school offered it, I wouldn't take it, for the following reasons:

Children who are two-and-a-half to four years old still need to be in car seats. Converted vans, which are used for fewer than twenty-four passengers and are what nursery schools use, don't have car seats. Even if they did, there would be no guarantee that the child would be strapped in properly.

I would be concerned that my child, at the end of the ride, might not know where to go. Suppose she or he saw a butterfly and chased after it. Not good. I do not think one bus driver, even one bus driver and an assistant, could shepherd a large number of children into the individual classrooms.

I appreciate that such busing would save the Granny-Nanny time, and it would be cheaper, but to me, it's ducking a responsibility on the part of the Granny-Nanny. She should personally deliver that child into the hands of the nursery school teacher . . . and at the end of the school day, personally retrieve the child to retain the chain of custody.

By Regular School Bus

For up-to-date info here, we turned to Gay Hoff, retired safety director of a large suburban school district, teacher/certifier of school bus drivers, visiting in-school lecturer, and a school bus driver herself for years.

She points out that in her experience many parents know the rules regarding school buses, but grandparents rarely do. Her advice begins this way:

Before The Child Leaves Home:

• **No jackets with drawstring bottoms**. The plastic tabs or toggles at the end of the strings have been known to catch in the railings of the bus and/or the doors. In one case, this resulted in a child being dragged and killed under the rear tires.

• **Watch those key-chain ornaments on backpacks**. As a child walks down the aisle of the bus, they swing back and forth and can injure a seated child.

• If the child has **lunch or snacks in that backpack**, stress that they are **not to be eaten on the bus** for fear of choking.

• **Be sure shoelaces are tied** to avoid a child's tripping at any point on the bus trip.

• If it's winter, **make sure caps have pom-poms on the top**. Easier for the driver to see the child in the mirror.

Most school bus accidents happen not on the bus, but waiting at the bus stop. Fewer would occur if adults would stop gossiping and watch the children.

• **The child should arrive at the bus stop at least five minutes before the bus is to arrive.** Get all hugs and kisses out of the way before the bus arrives.

• **Do not allow children to bring balls**, Frisbees, and the like to play with while waiting for the bus. The first thing you know, the thing will go out into the street and someone will chase after it. You don't want to know what happens next.

• If you are waiting at the bus stop with the child, **do not allow any of the children to play hide and seek.** One of the favorite hiding places is behind a car. If the bus driver doesn't see him, he may be left behind or he may dart out into traffic to catch the bus—a bad scene any way you look at it.

• **Children should stand at least ten feet back from the curb** and at right angles to the bus stop.

• It is preferable that the **younger children sit in the first rows of seats,** the older ones in the back.

• **The children have to get into the bus by themselves.** By law, the driver cannot leave his seat . . . and a parent cannot enter the bus. You may lift the child up onto the first step but that's the extent of the help you can give.

On The Bus And Under Way
• **Children usually sit three to a seat** (eleven inches of butt room is allowed, which makes for close quarters).

• **There are no seat belts**—yes, yes, I know, we've had the need for seat belts drummed into our heads for so long we're brainwashed (or should that be belt-washed?). But the school districts have good reason for not using seat belts. First, children under fifty pounds should never use a seat belt. Second, there is no need for a belt. The way school buses are designed, they are so high off the ground that in a collision with a car, the car will slide under the bus. Seat backs are high and seats are placed close together to, in a sense, compartmentalize each threesome.

• There are still more reasons for not having them: how does the driver of an eighty-four-passenger school bus enforce the wearing of them? And if they are worn (some school districts have experimented with them), what happens if the seat belt doesn't release in the case of an accident? Since there are no shoulder harnesses, great pressure is put on the pelvis of the child, which can cause physical damage, and many children will experience whiplash.

• The final reason is that children and seat belts can be a combustible combination. On one end of that seat belt is a heavy buckle and a ready-made weapon for walloping a seat mate—who will undoubtedly reciprocate.

• **Children should remain seated until the bus comes to a complete stop.** If they must cross the street to get to their home, they should watch for permission from the driver, who, sitting up high, can see any potential traffic hazards. Those flashing lights and the red stop signs and even the protective gates are no guarantee that oncoming drivers will stop. In truth, many won't and don't.

• **A child's best guarantee of safety is to listen to and respect the bus driver.**

Special Education Students

By law, children with disabilities are entitled to an education. Special buses are provided for their needs. These will have wheelchair lifts to bring the child up to floor level. It is up to the driver's assistant to put the wheelchair on the lift, raise it, roll the chair into place, and then tie down each chair so that it can't move. On these buses, seat belts and shoulder belts are provided because the buses themselves are smaller and not as collision-proof as their yellow bigger brothers.

Finally, by car.

Cars

Two facts that you should know:

1. Motor vehicle crashes are the leading cause of unintentional injury-related death among children fourteen and under.

2. One out of five grandparents never uses a child safety seat when transporting children under eight.

Enough said?

Car Seats

> If it is a car seat, it must not be ridden in until it has been protested with arched back and kicking feet.
> —Toddler Rules

Modern car seats for children are a must. The newest models are way safer than those from just a few years ago. By law they are to be used in the back seat only. The law varies by state as to how old the child must be before abandoning the car seat and switching to booster seats and then to regular seat belts. Infant seats should be placed so that the baby faces the rear of the car. After the child is a year old or has achieved twenty pounds in weight, the seat can be positioned so that the child faces forward.

You will need to change to larger car seats as your grandchildren grow. That bar that comes down over the front to provide additional safety? It won't fit over a larger child's head. The straps that protect a younger child in case of accident are too short to use with an older child. Conversely, using a seat too large for the child permits too much jostling in the event of an accident. From car seats, the child graduates to booster seats and from there, at fifty pounds, to a regular seat belt—but still in the back seat. Over the years, you can figure on needing at least two car seats (not counting infant seats) plus the booster seat for a preschool child. To find out exactly what type of car seat you need, go to the "car seat locator" at www.safekids.org/buckleup/index.cfm.

Fine, we're all in agreement on the use of car seats. Now, for the tricky part—installing them. Unfortunately there isn't one uniform set of directions because each car seat is unique. Once you get the car seat positioned, the next thing is to get the child in place. And that ain't easy. Besides dealing with a generally uncooperative passenger, you'll find the straps and buckles and snaps and padding and overhead bar very confusing. And then there's the arthritic thumb —yours of course—that has to fasten and unfasten those blasted catches.

Get good instructions from the parents or the manufacturer and practice, practice, practice. There's little that's more frustrating than finding yourself at nursery school with a crying granddaughter while you're unable to figure out how to strap her in for the trip home. Those young mothers watching you with amusement don't make it any easier, either.

To help ensure that child seat belts are operating properly, General Motors and the National SAFE KIDS Campaign organization have conducted the SAFE KIDS BUCKLE UP program since 1996. More than a quarter of a million seats have been checked nationwide under this program. In addition, SAFE KIDS coalitions across the country use Mobile Car Seat Check Up Vans to take the child safety message directly to local communities.

Free Safety Seats

Low-income families in thirty-seven states now participate in a program that provides thousands of free child safety seats through the generosity and help of the National SAFE KIDS Campaign, the international UAW union, General Motors, and the NAACP.

The program was begun in 1998 when UAW and GM pledged $5 million to the America's Promise initiative to purchase child safety seats for families in need. Well over 100,000 seats have been distributed through the NAACP and the National Council of La Raza, a program partner serving the Hispanic community.

Okay, everyone's buckled up, and you're on your way, and comes a wail from the back seat. Heartattacksville! What's going on back there? Choking or strangling could take less time than it takes you to bring the car to a halt, unbuckle your own seat belt, open the doors, and respond to the child's peril. Think ahead. Safety first is the right rule. No food or small toys in the back seat. It also helps if you invest in a safety mirror that allows you to check on the passengers in your back seat. It fits on the stem of your rearview mirror, about where you hang your handicapped sign. Unfortunately, not all mirrors fit on all automobiles so check it out before you buy.

Leave No Child Behind

Now all you have to do is get to your destination and remember to take the child out of the car seat. Piece of cake, you think. It's not. A 1998 analysis of fourteen child deaths due to hyperthermia had one refrain running through all the descriptions: she forgot…he forgot…they forgot. And in every one of these cases, it was a young person who forgot. That wasn't true in 2002 and 2003 and 2004, when more children died from hyperthermia because grandparents forgot and left their grandchildren unattended in a car. Why so? Sheer forgetfulness combined with the fact that there are more grandparents currently involved with caring for their grandchildren than there were in 1998.

If you Google on "grandfather + forgot + child + car + death + heat," you'll get nearly 14,800 responses in 0.48 seconds. Granted, many are duplicates, but too many aren't. The fact is that children are dying horrible deaths because of forgetfulness on the part of adults. And we grandparents have less excuse than others. How many times have you complained about having a Senior Moment or being afflicted with C.R.S. (Can't Remember S---!) or being memory-challenged or suffering from Halfzheimers or whatever you want to call plain old sheer forgetfulness?

The fact is that we dare not leave a child inside a vehicle even for a few minutes—it's the law in some states. It's common sense in every state.

"Cool temperatures are deceiving. If the temperature outside is between 70 and 80 degrees, within ten to fifteen minutes, the temperature inside a closed car is between 90 and 100 degrees," says Dr. Robin Foster, director of pediatric emergency services at the Medical College of Virginia Medical Center and head of the Child Protective Team. "In an hour, the car's inside temperature could be as high as 140 to 150 degrees."

A Cautionary Tale

Speaking of cars, the babysitter of last resort for some mothers is the auto-mobile. Let me tell you the story of one such mother:

A young woman who had lost her job and could not find any kind of day care, much less an affordable kind, finally accepted a temporary job that had a parking lot directly alongside the building. She stocked the car with toys and beverages, parked in the shade, cracked the windows all around, kissed her child bye-bye, and went to work. When she came out to check on her child one and a half hours later, it was too late, the child was dead.

This is a horrific tale. But not an uncommon one. If you go through any newspaper archive or visit www.kidsandcars.org/bottom_incidents.html on the Internet, you can read similar stories.

It is not enough to crack a window. According to the Department of Geosciences at San Francisco State University, car-heat studies show that within an hour, even with a window opened slightly, a car's inside temperature still rises about 45 to 50 degrees.

Have I really got you scared? I am too because I know I am forgetful...what's more my children know it too. They got me interested in Kids and Cars, a Kansas-based watchdog group that monitors vehicle-related child deaths (913-327-0013; email@kidsandcars.org).

Between Janette Fennell, president of Kids and Cars, and myself, we came up with the following tips:

• (I think this is the best one going.) Keep a large teddy bear in the child's car seat when it's not occupied. When the child is placed in the seat, put the teddy bear in the front passenger seat. It's a visual reminder of where your child is.

The rest require that you remember something . . . and the problem is, you have memory problems. On the other hand, if the child is old enough, your nannikin can remind you of one or more of the tips.

• Put something you'll need—like your cell phone, purse, wallet, reading glasses, lunch, or briefcase—on the back-seat floorboard. That way, you will see the child when you retrieve the object.

• Get in the habit of always opening the back door of your vehicle every time you reach your destination.

• If you have a rear fold-down seat, keep it closed so that a child can't crawl into the trunk.

• Get a window flag and fasten it onto the rear window whenever a child is in the back seat.

• If you use a sunshade on the child's side, make sure you can see through it clearly; otherwise it may obscure your vision of the child.

And there's something that we all can do:

• **If you see a child alone in a vehicle, get involved. If the child is hot or seems sick, try to remove him from the car as quickly as possible. Call 911 immediately.**

CHAPTER 10

Emergency Preparedness

As a Granny-Nanny, you must be prepared
to face any emergency. That means doing certain things
in advance so that your reaction
can be swift and sure.

Medical Procedures

Master the Heimlich maneuver and CPR. Don't know how to do them? Take a course and hope that you never have to use the knowledge. You can also memorize the instructions given for choking, at www.heimlichinstitute.org/howtodo.html.

In Case Of Fire...

Be prepared for a house fire. Sure, the odds are slim that your residence or the child's home will be involved, but you never know. That's why there are fire companies. So what do you do in advance?

• Post the local fire company's number somewhere prominent.

• Write up the fastest route to the residence and post that, too.

• Let everyone know where you posted this information.

• Put up smoke detectors in recommended places and change the batteries twice a year. Test one so everyone will recognize the sound.

• Buy a fire extinguisher for small fires.

• Make sure existing extinguishers are in good operating condition, and that the adults know how to use them.

• Remember that putting water on a grease fire is a no-no and that mixing water and electricity can be dangerous.

• Keep matches and lighters out of sight and out of reach.

• Teach all children of sufficient age what to do in case of a fire. For example, tell them to get out and stay out. Toys can be replaced... people can't.

• Tell children not to try to put out the fire themselves. It just wastes time.

• Have them call 911 from a neighbor's house.

• Show them how to close doors between the fire and the rest of the house.

• Insist that they sleep with bedroom doors closed.

• Demonstrate how to detect fire behind a door by feeling the door with the back of the hand.

• Show how to stay low to the floor as they escape the fire because the heat and smoke are more intense higher up.

• Teach them how to stop, drop, and roll if their clothing is on fire.

• Show them in pictures, or if possible in person, what a fireman in full uniform looks like (maybe a trip to the local fire company is in order).

Other Emergencies

• Ask the child's doctor about emergency procedures in the event of allergic reactions to food or insect stings. The pediatrician will advise what medicines to have on hand.

• The same goes for food poisoning. There was a time when it was thought that having syrup of ipecac on hand was enough. Today's guidelines are different. Check.

• If you have a swimming pool, take precautions that will keep toddlers away from the pool.

• Encourage parents to teach their children to swim at an early age, even before they are a year old.

• Firearms in the house require special attention with little ones around. Keep all firearms in locked cabinets or closets. **Store them unloaded!!! And lock the ammo in another, separate place!**

It cannot be said too often: The number-one killer of children is not disease, violence, or crime, but **unintentional injury**. As a Granny-Nanny, you have a clear responsibility to make your grandchildren's environment as safe as possible. Prevention of accidents—falls, cuts, burns, poisonings, eye injuries, etc.—is your first line of defense. Knowing what to do and what remedies to use when something happens is equally important.

PART IV

Talk, Talk, Talk

It is a common delusion that you make things better
by talking about them.

—Dame Rose Macaulay, *The Towers of Trebizond*

Dame Rose (1881–1958) may have been right: talking per se does not have a good name. Which is probably why so many child care books devote so much time to the finding and hiring of child care providers and so little space to retaining them. As mentioned in Chapter 2, one such book spent 96 percent of its space on the process of getting a nanny and 4 percent on keeping her (which, when you come right down to it, requires a certain amount of talking with her).

When it comes to Granny-Nannies, the reverse is true. Ninety-six percent of making it work is the result of talking, the other 4 percent is luck, fate, whatever you want to call it.

So, let's talk the talk (which high-paid professionals call "communicating").

CHAPTER 11

Too Much Of A Good Thing: Which Granny-Nanny?

The hardest thing in life to learn is
which bridge to cross and which to burn.

—David Russell

Life is not a continuum of pleasant choices,
but of inevitable problems that call for strength,
determination, and hard work.

—Proverb

One of the advantages of getting married is that you usually bring two sets of potential Granny-Nannies (a.k.a. in-laws) to the wedding. Therefore, when it comes time to choose someone to watch your child, you may actually have a choice. In fact, a surfeit of choices if there are step-grandparents involved. In other words, all the grandparents step forward and volunteer. (We should all have such problems.)

Needless to say, this can be potentially dangerous since some noses are going to be out of joint . . . maybe permanently. So, although the mother usually does the choosing, for the sake of amiability and holiday get-togethers, get your own act together as partners and parents, come up with coherent noninflammatory reasons for your decision, and speak as one. You both made the choice, you both think it's the right one. **(Beware! Do not make the mistake of hinting that it was your spouse's decision, which can have repercussions down the line!—especially if you decide to change Granny-Nannies later.)**

Then there are families in which there is only one Granny-Nanny choice, or sometimes none at all. If you do not have the resources financially to go in another direction and thus "not impose on her" (that's your out), you have to suck it up and make the best of it. Sometimes things really do work out for the best, maybe because everyone is trying harder. Parents who have only that one choice will probably be green with jealousy of parents with multiple choices. They shouldn't be. Choosing between Granny-Nannies is a process filled with land mines.

So, how to choose? Begin by analyzing yourself. If you cannot speak to your mother-in-law without cringing, you probably should not ask her to be your child's Granny-Nanny. However, strangely enough, based on interviews I've conducted, about 60 percent of the most successful relationships involve mothers-in-law —perhaps because each walks skittishly around the other, trying not to offend. Also, there is a spouse waiting in the wings to intervene. Of course, once that happens, all bets are off! It becomes a variation on the eternal triangle, and you know how that works out, with two parties taking sides against the third, and the sides changing all the time. For example, one daughter-in-law advises, "Always address all concerns to each other directly, because every time she tried to talk to my husband about it, he would make her more upset somehow. And I was REALLY mad hearing how much she was talking about me behind my back."

Okay, what about your own mother? If you and your mother argue about every little thing and have since childhood, what makes you think this won't continue when a child is involved? On the other hand, it is certainly easier to talk to your own parent about large and small concerns. Chances are you and she share the same principles of mothering, too. And the best reason you might prefer her, arguments and all, is that you did manage to grow to adulthood under her care and you turned out pretty well, didn't you?

I do want to assure you that I found numerous mother-in-law/daughter-in-law and mother/daughter relationships that on the surface appear to be disasters, but they work. For example, one mother said, "My mother-in-law and I do not get along, but my husband and I discussed all of the positive and negative points and decided that it is in the best interest of our daughter to stay with my mother-in-law." That's because the care of the child supersedes all else.

One mother who had had both her mother-in-law and her mother care for her child at different times said, "I realized that they [her mother-in-law and mother] have different mothering techniques than I do, so of course they are going to do a few things differently than me. And I am going to disagree with them from time to time, but I feel that pales in comparison to making sure my two babies are being loved and hugged all day long by someone who is not paid to do it!"

Okay, you've made your choice between the two possibilities. How do you break the news to the loser?

You are going to have to find a logical, factual reason to select one over the other (location, size of home, proximity to pediatrician and/or hospital, age or health of grandparents). If all else is equal, then an "I feel more comfortable with my mother" might work, but unless you want to cause a family feud, don't use that idea on your mother (i.e., "I feel more comfortable with my mother-in-law"). Watch out when the shooting starts. Or, try dividing the time between grandparents, if two sets are available. Although on the surface this looks like a winner, it's not always the best for the children since they will be facing three sets of rules, in fact three of everything.

Once the choice is made, things may not be as clear-cut as you think. Instead, you may face balancing problems. For example, "My mother-in-law has offered to watch our newborn next year while I return to work for a couple days during the week. Even though it hasn't been hashed out with my boss, my hope is to work two days in the office and three days from home. My worry is that my mom will feel a little 'left behind' while my mother-in-law will get to see the baby every other day, and my mom won't. I know we'll have to make an extra effort to visit Grandma and Grandpa when we can so it's as balanced as it could be. . . . My mom works full time so there's no way they could switch off from time to time. My husband's mom doesn't work at all so it's definitely more convenient for her."

Speaking about feeling left behind, a mother brought up an aspect of Granny-Nannying that never occurred to me: favoritism. It is only natural that when one sees a grandchild three, four, or five days a week, a special relationship develops. But how about the other grandchildren? As one mother noted, "Please consider the feelings of your other grandchildren, whom you do not watch. My child is almost completely ignored by her grandmother because the grandmother is so involved in her other grandchild. The other grandchild walks around Granny's house telling my child that all the toys are hers, and the bed is hers, and the special cup, plate, and utensils are hers. My child feels so left out."

Please remember that when the child walks out the door with his or her parents, then your job is done for the day. Done. Terminado. Except for answering phone calls about what may or may not have happened during the day. A word to the wise—many mothers warn about Granny-Nannies intruding in birthday parties or holiday celebrations. "These are the parents' times. We're there. We can take care of the child," one said, then added, "and we don't need her 'cause she doesn't know how to stop Granny-Nannying." Pretty strong hint, wouldn't you say?

CHAPTER 12

Your Place Or Mine?

Logistics trump everything.

—Computer genius David Platt's Third Law of the Universe

If Granny-Nanny lives along your route to work, it's logical to take the child to her. And, on the other hand, if she lives miles away from your job and in the opposite direction, it makes more sense to have her come to your house. (There is one exception, which involves state aid—to be discussed in Chapter 13, Money Matters, page 99.) However, convenience is not always the clincher. There are Granny-Nannies in New York and other metropolitan areas who take a subway and then a bus to get to their grandchildren's homes—long round trips they are glad to make.

The type of home may be an important factor, especially if the physical strength and agility of a Granny-Nanny come into play. If one or both of the homes is two-story, alterations have to be made. Carrying a baby in one hand and helping a toddler navigate stairs can be dangerous for all concerned. In the best of all possible worlds, a ranch house is the ideal setting for a Granny-Nanny and her charges—but for those who live in two-story houses, here are some quick changes that can be made:

• Turn your sideboard into a changing table. Diapers can go in drawers, lotions and bottles into compartments.

• Turn the most unused room in the place (usually the dining room) into a dormitory with portacribs or futons or sleeping bags or cots that can fold up and be put away after nap time.

• Make your powder room into a potty room. It's closer and accidents are less apt to happen than if you try to get upstairs fast.

• Supply a stool to give youngsters access to toothbrushes and the like—just make sure the stool won't tip over if weight is put on the edge instead of the center.

• Put a gate across the bottom of the stairs so that access to the second floor can be controlled.

• Keep all doors to the outside locked and install special childproof locks if necessary.

• Put your precious Oriental rugs into storage upstairs until spills are at a minimum and tripping is not a hazard.

This won't work for you? Can't sleep everybody on one floor?

• Use monitors in bedrooms for nap time to avoid making unnecessary trips upstairs.

Granny-Nanny's Home

If everything is equal, then personal preferences come into play. Some Granny-Nannies want or need to do things while simultaneously keeping an eye on a child. For them, nap time represents free time to take care of their own home or personal needs. For example, I live 150 yards from my grandchildren's home. I could easily have gone to them. Instead I opted to have my grandchildren come to me so I could write this book.

Although my son and daughter-in-law have the very latest in computers (both are in the tech business), it would have meant carrying disks back and forth, having duplicate hard-copy research materials, and so on. For me, my house (no stairs!!!) was the logical solution. However, the downside was that doing the child care thing at Granny's requires some duplication of furnishings. Since it was my idea for the children to come to my house, and I had the space and could afford it, I thought it was only fair that I supply the big basic stuff (crib, mattress, high chair, playpen, and the like). This may not be true for other Granny-Nannies. In any event, the little stuff is another matter. Who furnishes the diapers, the food, the toys, etc.? It should be noted that the average grandparent spends an average of $500 per year on each grandchild. In the case of a Granny-Nanny, there's no reason some of that money couldn't go to food, toys, books, and the like.

While preferences should be taken into consideration, many parents have another perspective on whether the child goes to Granny, based on concerns about such things as the presence of cats and dogs, whether the house can be childproofed, potential breakage of valuable objects by children, how the dishes are washed (dog-licking is a no-no), and even basic cleanliness. Obviously, accommodations are going to have to be made here, for example, smoke detectors supplied or child gates installed. And that's just the start.

What about the accommodations children have to make—always being aroused in time to go to Grandmother's, never allowed to sleep in, even after a bad night. Then, again, many children like to have a change of toys from one house to the next. And fortunately, most children are flexible . . . about certain things. Not about others, but we'll get to that in a moment.

The Child's Home

Other Granny-Nannies opt to watch a child in the child's own home because that is where clothes and toys are. (Plus, it keeps Granny-Nannies' homes from having to be as "kid-friendly.")

Some parents worry about . . .

• Snooping grannies who go through things they shouldn't or find things they shouldn't.

• Grannies breaking or ruining things.

• Grannies turning up the thermostat because they like it warmer, which boosts fuel bills.

• Grannies answering the phone when they've been asked not to, or signing for packages or letting in strangers.

• Grannies overusing the phone, including making long-distance calls.

• Grannies serving for lunch a meal planned for that night's dinner, leaving Mother to scramble together something to eat when she comes home.

• Grannies using up all the milk and other basics, which means a hurried trip to the store to restock.

Neatness and cleanliness come into play here, also. Mommy may not want to come home to a messy house, or one that has been cleaned the wrong way (meaning not the way Mommy would clean it). Or a home that has been rearranged...even inadvertently. A leftie may put things in one place, a rightie in another. On the other hand, a parent may expect some chores to be done around the house ("after all, the child's napping and she has free time"), which is a no-no. At least the expecting part. If a Granny-Nanny chooses to load the dishwasher or fold the laundry or pick up some things, that's a bonus and should be received gratefully as a gift.

Remember, like a hired nanny, your Granny-Nanny is there to care for the child, not for the house.

One prospective Granny-Nanny told me, "They want me to move in and take care of my granddaughter. At least, that's what they say. Actually, they want me there to do the picking up and cleaning and everything else. I love my grandchild, but I won't do it."

It is also true that some Granny-Nannies will willingly do the shopping and run errands, like picking up the dry-cleaning, just as an opportunity to get out of the house and be able to talk to someone without bending over. Which brings up the question of whose car to use, should one be needed. If you want her to use her own, reimbursement for gas is in order. She may say no, in which case filling her gas tank once in a while will pay dividends.

One young mother brought up the subject of falls. If Granny falls at her own house, it is covered by her homeowner's insurance. If it happens at the children's house, her insurance may not cover it. Ditto the situation in the event a child falls. It's something to check out.

Another point, made by a Granny-Nanny, was a problem with the newfangled phones. In the old days, when the telephone company supplied the phones, the phone number was displayed prominently on each phone. The new portable ones don't have that display. In an emergency, Granny-Nanny may not remember her grandchildren's home phone number. This makes it incumbent on the parent to post the phone number on each phone as well as posting a list of important numbers near each phone.

Posted phone numbers should include:

Parents' work numbers

Parents' cell phone numbers (I don't know about you, but I always have to look them up.)

Pediatrician's phone number

Dentist's phone number

Poison Control Center 1-800-222-1222

Local fire company

Local police department

Local ambulance company

School phone number

School snow phone number

CHAPTER 13

Money Matters

It sometimes happens, even in the best of families,
that a baby is born. This is not necessarily
cause for alarm. The important thing is to keep your wits
about you and borrow some money.

—Elinor Goulding Smith

Who Pays For All That Stuff?

When I volunteered to care for my grandchildren at my house, I had no idea about what costs were involved. I confess to being shocked out of my gourd. I mean the bumper was beautiful, colorful, well made, and all that—but $300?

Before we began our awfully big adventure in shopping for baby and children's equipment, we consulted various books and websites, such as Google's www.froogle.com, a website for discounted brand-name items, as resources. We had but two criteria: we didn't care how anything looked so long as it was safe . . . and cheap. Oh, yes, and we used the Internet to determine which high chairs, cribs, walkers, playpens, etc., were safe and hadn't been recalled by the U.S. Consumer Product Safety Commission.

And the cribs, that was a real lollapalooza! We spent a lot of time on those. Iron cribs. Round cribs. Canopy cribs. Hand-painted cribs. Cribs in the form of bunny rabbits. Cribs with a nautical or garden theme. Cribs that cost $500 and up? Outrageous. (Although I confess to being tempted by a crib that converted into a day bed and later an adult bed. Then, I figured out that I could buy all three pieces for less than the original, and I wouldn't have to disassemble and assemble in the process.)

So off to the discount stores (Froogle is a handy reference) and another rude awakening: as one Internet retailer noted, "Discount baby furniture is sometimes difficult to come by since it seems that anything to do with a baby instantly means a very high price tag."

This was not for me. Not for the mom who wrote a genre-starting child care book, the first to explore childrearing from a financial point of view: *How to Bring Up a Child Without Spending a Fortune* (David McKay, 1972).

Out of desperation, as new Granny-Nannies, my husband and I became shopaholics. Every Friday night we studied the garage sales in the classifieds. The words "baby furniture" galvanized us into action. We checked addresses against a map, drew up a route, and made sure we had cash on hand since many garage-sale people won't take checks. And we were successful. Our best crib buy, however, was made at an impulsive stop at a garage sale miles from home. The crib was made of teak and cost $100 (including the mattress, which we replaced with a new one for health reasons). We later saw the same crib in a baby store for $700.

Besides garage sales, we haunted every thrift store and Salvation Army and Goodwill outlet in the area. On longer trips, the word "thrift" on any sign brought our car to a sudden halt. Our baby buys covered parts of three states.

The only piece we didn't have to buy was a bassinet; we brought that down from the attic, where it had sat from the days when our son fit into it.

The only bad buy came from a department store, a reputable one. It was a rocker-glider from a famous name. We ended up reporting it to the Product Safety Commission and got back our money—which we promptly spent buying another rocker-glider.

It was a rude awakening to discover that not only are all things baby made of plastic (except the kids themselves), but that they also are musical or make weird, loud sounds, and don't do a thing without batteries. Talk about cost; if we had a nickel for every toy battery we've bought, we could probably buy a new TV.

However, we can't complain too much. Remember, all this was our choice. We had chosen to have the child come to us and not vice versa. The cost of the heater for the baby wipes was another story.

What's A Granny-Nanny Worth?

Of all the concerns involving Granny-Nannying, money matters rank either right at the top or right at the bottom. As one Granny-Nanny put it, "I'd pay to have the opportunity to take care of my grandchild." And it is a matter of record that fewer than 15 percent of grandparents are paid for their child care.

Said one mother, "My husband and I haven't discussed paying his mom at all, but I'm sure we'll want to. She'd have to drive an hour to get to our house to watch him (we JUST learned this week it's a boy!), so we'd feel it would be right to pay her something. What? I don't know!"

Here are some responses:

"I pay $250 a week, which is $1,000 a month for just my daughter."

"I had found a home day care center that only had one other baby. I paid $120 per week. I couldn't drop him off before 6:30 A.M. and had to pick him up by 5:30 P.M., otherwise I was charged $10 per fifteen-minute increment thereafter... [She had other problems, too]... My husband and I decided to get a newer, safer, more economical car and drove eighty miles each day to my parents' home. I paid them the same $120 per week and didn't worry about rushing to pick him up or whether he was taken care of ... We've finally purchased our first home three blocks away from them."

"I pay my mom $20 a day—$100 per week when I work a full week. It seems to be enough for her without putting me in a hole."

"My dad watched my son from the time he was four months until he was thirteen months and he charged me $10 a day. He said that it was his privilege to be able to watch his grandson, and getting to know the child was great."

"My mother watches my fifteen-month-old son when I work, which varies day to day . . . I don't pay her, but if I can help with any household items or gas for the car I do. As well when I shop, I ask her if there is anything she needs and I pay for it. It's great and I'm really fortunate."

As you can see, the payments vary all over the lot. What the Granny-Nanny is paid depends a great deal on the finances of both the grandparents and the parents. If the former are doing it to help out the latter financially, the payment, if any, will be small. On the other hand, if the parents are well-heeled, they could pay top dollar.

Generally speaking, Granny-Nannies who are paid receive approximately half of what the same service would cost at a child care center. However, there are other factors to consider that are built into most child care center costs: food, diapers, equipment, toys; arts and crafts stuff; child safety equipment; playpens; educational videotapes. (On the other hand, it may surprise you to discover that at some of the most prestigious nursery schools, the parents are supposed to supply diapers, toilet paper, and paper towels so as to keep costs down.)

As the Granny-Nanny, it is not unreasonable to expect that you should receive at least the same things a prestigious nursery school expects. And if you're doing it for free, it is not unreasonable to expect more. But that is a matter for discussion between you and the parents.

Legalities

What about tax returns and the like? Insurance costs and ambulance services?

If Granny-Nanny cares for the grandchild in her own home for free, and if she has a family ambulance plan, the child is covered by that plan—but be sure to check this out in your state. Likewise, if anything happens to the child at Granny-Nanny's, the medical portion of her homeowner's will kick in.

But if the Granny-Nanny is paid, a separate rider for the insurance policy has to be bought and paid for. And you will probably have to negotiate with the ambulance company to see if they have a plan that will cover the situation. Please note, once upon a time all health insurance policies covered at least part of the costs of an ambulance, but this may not be true anymore. So be sure to check health insurance policies as well.

Taxes are a different story. Now, I am not an accountant so instead of taking my word on this, consult your tax preparer. However, according to the Social Security Administration, by law, if you pay a household worker (including your child who is twenty-one or older) $1,400 or more in cash wages during the year, the wages are subject to Social Security withholding and matching payments. That sounds like a lot of money, but it works out to slightly in excess of $25 a week—not a whole lot of money.

When it comes to paying for child care, there are many things to consider, including, strangely enough, how old the Granny-Nanny is. Up to age seventy, every dollar reported to the Social Security Administration will reduce her Social Security payment by fifty cents. After age seventy, she can earn as much as she likes.

But if your child is in child care (and this has been interpreted to include your Granny-Nanny's home) you may be eligible for a child and dependent care tax credit. According to the Child Care Aware Center (which is partially sponsored by the Child Care Bureau of the U.S. Department of Health and Human Services.), this tax credit has several requirements. However, if you do qualify for this credit, you can deduct a lot of your child care or dependent care expenses.

This Credit Is Best For:

• Working parents (both parents have to work) with children under the age of thirteen who are in child care or in an after-school care program.

• One parent who works while the other parent is a full-time student who doesn't work, and they have children under the age of thirteen who are in child care or in an after-school care program.

To Receive This Credit You Must:

• Work and earn enough to be taxed on that income.

• Pay for the care of a dependent: a child under thirteen years old, a spouse with a disability, or a parent who needs care while you are at work.

DON'T MAKE THIS MISTAKE: In the year 2000, over 600,000 families did not take advantage of $238 million in tax refunds for the Child Tax Credit.

In addition, twenty-six states plus the District of Columbia currently have their own child care and dependent care credit. If the state that you live in has this credit, you can file for it both in your state and federal taxes. Contact your state tax or revenue office for more information on this.

Furthermore, you may be entitled to child care assistance. Contact your state child care subsidy agency. Or, if you have access to the Internet, go to nccic.org/state data/statepro/index.html. Look for "State Profiles" on the National Child Care Information Center's website. Find yours and click for more info.

It may be that your payments for child care and your tax credits and care assistance will balance out. Again, consult a tax expert on this.

It also may be that when your Granny-Nanny figures out what your payments are going to mean to her financially, she will opt out of being paid. Of course, you won't get the child care tax credit, but you'll be getting the best child care available for free.

On the other hand, when one is getting a freebie, one has certain obligations, such as not taking advantage of the situation. If you are due home at a certain hour, be there—unless you call first and explain extenuating circumstances.

Some parents choose to reimburse the Granny-Nanny in other ways—gift certificates to restaurants or bringing home flowers or doing chores around the house or paying for a cleaning woman. One set of parents actually paid for a cruise for the grandparents and another gave theirs airplane tickets to England.

If you want to spend money on something that will benefit everyone—parents, grandparents, and children—consider enrolling your child in a half-day nursery school (covered in the next chapter). It gives the Granny-Nanny some time out; it gives parents assurance that, at least on nursery school days, the child is in a structured, physically active environment and will learn to play with a peer group.

There is one perfect way to compensate a Granny-Nanny, and it doesn't cost a cent: an occasional heartfelt thank-you goes a long way. And you don't even have to buy a card. Of course, a filet mignon dinner—your treat—doesn't hurt either, and you'll get a chance to discuss the wonderful things your child is accomplishing.

CHAPTER 14

Teacher's Pets

Education is what remains after one has forgotten
what one has learned in school.

—John Dryden

If you can afford it, and if you can wangle your way into a good nursery school or preschool, this is one way to get all the advantages of both a Granny-Nanny and an educational child care setting.

Nursery schools have been around for a long, long time. Preschools are newer and seem to have come into existence about the time of the Head Start program in public schools.

What's the difference between them? Not much, other than, occasionally, different philosophies. Both operate for two to three hours per day, two to five days a week, during the school year. One big difference is the ages of attendees. Traditionally, nursery schools take two-to-four-year-olds, and preschools three-to-four-year-olds. But this differs around the country, and often the names have become interchangeable. However, a word to the status-conscious. As one mother put it, "Nursery school is the first step to going to an Ivy League college."

Since we're not into preparing for college yet but only trying to get through early childhood into grade school, our question has to be: would any form of early childhood education be of benefit to the child and the grandparent?

Should You/Shouldn't You Go The Nursery School Route?

Should

If your child has little or no contact with children her own age and instead lives in a totally adult environment, she may need the socializing she gets at school. It may be that you will have to look for a school with smaller classes to compensate.

Speaking of an adult-only environment, it can be pretty dull for a youngster unless there is a constant inflow of new toys or an awful lot of TV watching. A school where the creativity of playmates and the enthusiasm of teachers make old toys seem new can be a great compensation for aging grandparents.

Learning to share the attention of a teacher with six or seven others is also beneficial . . . not to mention the freedom of not being constantly under the watchful eye of a single adult.

Learning, of course, is the name of the game here, and both you and Granny-Nanny may be surprised at some of the things these children learn—and no, I'm not talking about playing doctor. Computers in a class of three-year-olds are not unusual.

What's in it for Granny-Nanny? A couple of hours for herself in the morning. Add that to nap time in the afternoon, and she may not know what to do with all her time. Yes, yes, I'm only kidding.

Shouldn't

If your child treats your departure each day as absolute, total desertion, he may not be up to separating from his Granny-Nanny. However, most teachers at such schools are prepared for reluctant attendees and quickly involve them in exciting activities.

You also shouldn't go the nursery school route if you are concerned about disease. One of the advantages of Granny-Nannying for children is that there's less exposure to germs than at a child care center. Now, we're talking colds, flu, infectious diseases, head lice, and the like.

If you or the Granny-Nanny shudder at the thought, you may want to postpone organized child care until the child is ready for prekindergarten. At that point, I do think it is a good idea. For one thing, the child who is never exposed to a cold during his preschool years is going to be sick continuously during his first year of regular schooling, and that's an educational handicap he may have difficulty overcoming.

Another consideration is the cost. Nursery schools and preschools are expensive. Not so much as full-time child care centers, but nobody's giving space away for free.

Nor are there any scholarships available. Furthermore, the best schools have waiting lists. You've heard of parents enrolling their children in college at birth? No longer, not in this competitive day and age—but enrolling them in nursery school the day after they're born? That happens.

How To Transport That Child To The School (Assuming You Can't Walk There)?

I am unaware of any of these schools providing transportation. It is possible in small close-knit communities or in cities that busing will be available, but even if it were, I wouldn't use it. (See my reservations on page 76.)

If it's Granny-Nanny in her invisible chauffeur's cap, two round trips a day can add up in terms of time and gasoline. However, it may be worth it to her to have a respite in the morning. In fact, I know of one Granny-Nanny who offered to not only do the driving but pay the tuition as well. One thing that should be checked is whether her automobile insurance is sufficient under the circumstances. Also, we're talking duplicate car seats, unless you're going to transfer the seats back and forth between cars.

What Type Of School?

If cost and distance are of no concern, then you may want to explore some of the many choices open to you.

Many of the schools with better reputations are connected to churches, since they can benefit from a nonprofit status. Nor do they need to be licensed in most states. However, they frequently have a board of overseers composed of parishioners who take a keen interest in the school since their children or grandchildren go there or have gone there.

Which brings up the question of what to do when it's the wrong religion. My response is: enroll now, ask later. Once you have a place held for you, find out just how much religious indoctrination takes place. The only nod to religious instruction may be saying a nondenominational grace before snacks.

But, setting aside religion, is a generic nursery school what you really want for your child? Maybe you want a school that will teach your child to read . . . or one that will emphasize learning through play (which is the most modern approach and espoused by the National Association for the Education of Young Children) . . . or a program that is based on a particular philosophy. The most famous and oldest of these are the Montessori schools . . . the newest are those using High/Scope curricula . . . and the fastest spreading are the Waldorf schools.

Reading instruction in nursery schools has gone out of vogue since academic learning programs simply didn't work in the vast majority of cases. Yes, you can still find them, but you may have to travel a distance to get to one.

Whichever you choose, it's a good idea to get input from Granny-Nanny. Take her with you. Get her reaction. You both should be happy with your choice because it's awfully hard to change your mind later and switch schools. In fact, it is well-nigh impossible.

CHAPTER 15

Little Things Add Up

It has long been an axiom of mine
that the little things are infinitely
the most important.

—Sir Arthur Conan Doyle, creator of Sherlock Holmes

I remember watching a movie when I was a little girl (it was in black and white, of course) in which a French spy always crooked his little finger when drinking a cuppa. It drove the hero wild. I don't know why. Nor do I know why leaving the cap on or off the toothpaste is such a bone of contention in some marriages. I definitely do understand why leaving the toilet seat up can create a fracas.

The point is that little things can turn into big irritations. So the obvious thing to do is try to halt those little things before they get out of hand. As one mother noted, "So far, we have had two major fights about ridiculous things. In my opinion, they started because I said or did something, and instead of asking me about it right then, she [Granny-Nanny] let it build up inside and complained to everyone else and never came to me about it at all. In her opinion, she took my actions as ways of telling her that she wasn't doing a good job and got offended and frustrated."

So both you and the Granny-Nanny have to agree up front that if anything bothers either one of you, you'll sit down and discuss it like adults. (Be tactful—imagine she's the CEO of your company and in control of your future employment, which she is to some degree because you need her more than she needs you unless you're paying her big bucks.)

Some Possible Areas Of Contention

How Many Days?

Just as Granny-Nannies come in all sizes and all shapes and all ages and both genders, they also participate in a variety of scheduling arrangements. There are one-day-a-week Granny-Nannies. Recently, doctors have praised such an arrangement as giving parents a day of freedom to schedule appointments or attend meetings or you name it. I've met two-day-a-week and three-day-a-week Granny-Nannies who are enabling a parent to go back to school part time. Then there's the four-day-a-week Granny-Nannies (that's us!), who give the parent a means of maintaining a career. (And let me tell you how much we appreciate that one day a week off to schedule our own appointments.)

Of course, there are the full-time Granny-Nannies who work five, six, and sometimes seven days a week because circumstances demand it.

Flexibility, thy name is not Granny-Nanny!

The one thing that all those less-than-full-time Granny-Nannies advise is: be as inflexible as possible about the day or days to which you've agreed. If you're a one-day-a-weeker, pick your day and, except in emergencies, stick to it. Do not, those Granny-Nannies say, make it an open-ended arrangement. Plan accordingly. It is the "what day would you like this week?" Granny-Nanny who finds her one day has somehow mushroomed to two or even spread to three.

Remember, this is a two-way street: the Granny-Nanny is giving the parent a whole day or days of freedom; the parent is giving the Granny-Nanny the opportunity to know and love her nannikins.

Sounds pretty good to me; how about you?

Hours

When you take a job, you want to know what the days and hours are. So does the Granny-Nanny. If you say you'll be home each night by 6:30, you should do your darnedest (short of having an accident) to be there on time. If you can't, a phone call is in order. If you know in advance when you must stay late, she should be told immediately, in the event she has made plans. Granny-Nanny should not be the last one to know you're going on a trip.

And if at all possible, you must accommodate necessary occurrences in Granny-Nanny's life, such as her doctor's appointments, even if it means taking a sick day from work. If you discuss it in advance, she may be able to get an early morning or late afternoon appointment that will allow you to miss some time at work but make it up later. Employers are generally forgiving about such matters.

Expectations

This is ranked number one on some lists of topics to discuss (it is also called Do's and Don'ts). It is a booby trap in disguise for parents. If you show up with a list of wants and no-no's, you're in deep doo-doo. You are talking to a woman who has raised one or more kids. She may listen, but she won't take it well. So, here's where the real talking begins. (By the way, there's nothing wrong with making out a list, but commit it to memory and never show it to her. If you can't remember everything, put the list in your pocket and, if need be, excuse yourself to use the bathroom and refresh your memory.) Do not confuse this list of expectations with the nuts-and-bolts list of topics to be agreed upon at the end of this chapter. They ain't the same thing. Not by a long shot.

You may be surprised at the many potential areas of contention here—or you may not. For instance: Dr. Spock vs. Dr. Brazelton . . . ponytails vs. long hair . . . sleeper bags vs. footed sleepers . . . pacifiers vs. thumb-sucking . . . night-lights vs. darkness . . . bottle-feeding of solids vs. spooning it in . . . when to abandon bottles and go to sippy-cups . . . jelly on top of or under the peanut butter, about which we'll say more later.

One Granny-Nanny threw up her hands and announced, "What goes on behind my doors is my business." Another said, "You show me an adult who can't eat with a spoon and drink out of a cup, and I'll do it your way." I mean, you are talking major belligerence here!

A Report Card

Many child care centers give parents a daily report on each child (it's a computerized form), which notes how much the child ate, how much and when he slept, how he got along with other kids, whether he used bad words, etc.

It is understandable, then, that parents may feel (and Granny-Nannies may agree) that a report on the child is due at the end of the day. In fact, one young mother, when asked what she would do differently if she were just starting out with a Granny-Nanny, reported that she'd ask the Granny-Nanny to keep a journal. That way she'd know what and how much the child had to eat at what times . . . when and for how long she had napped . . . whether her bowels had moved, how often, and what consistency. Did she play inside and/or outside? Did she go anywhere? Did she use bad words?

And Where Did That Bruise Come From?

Of course, this last question is the most important, and it will be addressed fully in Chapter 18, Abuse (page 138).

Keeping a written journal might be a little more than your Granny-Nanny is up for—unless you provide your own form—but you can ask for a verbal report, which would be considered a normal request in any job. And it can come in handy when visiting the doctor.

Most Granny-Nannies will not object to making a verbal report, at the very least, especially if they can boast about some accomplishment of the child's (or of their own, like getting the kid to eat cream of rice or some other yucky food).

Of course, the Granny-Nanny deserves a similar report, either when she arrives at the child's home or when the parent drops a child off. It's important for the Granny-Nanny to know: did the child sleep well, is she sniffling, is she constipated, is she suffering from some emotional trauma, and so on.

One of the great advantages of such verbal reports is that they are a practical form of communicating. Mother and Granny-Nanny are talking about a subject in which they have a mutual interest! It is a start.

Major Points Of Disagreement

Number One: Schedules

Currently, there seems to be a reversion to the early days of the twentieth century, when children were supposed to eat at a certain time, nap at a certain time, bathe at a certain time, play at a certain time.

I own a book entitled *Motherhood*, published in 1918, which has a complete baby schedule down to exact times by the clock. A baby cries from hunger at 11:45 and is not scheduled for lunch until 12:00? Too bad, the baby waits. Crying was not on *Motherhood's* schedule, and mothers were advised to ignore it when it occurred. Psychiatrists and psychologists weighed in later to say that such rigid practices caused psychological problems in adulthood. Did it? Who knows.

Then the pendulum swung the other way. Permissiveness or demand-feeding was the thing in the mid-to-late twentieth century, aided by Dr. Spock (and his wife, who ghost-wrote his later books). If he's hungry, feed him. If he's crying, pick him up. If he fusses, something's wrong—investigate.

One parent showed up at Granny-Nanny's with a written schedule that the kids followed on the weekends: "Like when they had been napping and when they ate cereal—because I thought it might help her to have an idea of what to expect, and if they got fussy, she could see that maybe it was because they usually sleep at that time or eat cereal then. She took that as me saying she wasn't doing a good job, and I wanted her to put them on this strict schedule. She lost it and freaked out."

The Written Word Strikes Again!

You and the Granny-Nanny are going to have to arrive at some modus operandi here. My hunch is that Granny-Nannies are conditioned by training (and their feeling of obligation to their grandchildren's parents) to come a-running when a child cries. It also may be that the child's cries are harder for them to ignore or simply sound louder in a house where little is happening. Whatever the case, accept up front that a Granny-Nanny is not going to live by a strict schedule, not when a child is crying. But we all live to some degree on a schedule (the alarm clock in the A.M., lunch at noon, the end-of-shift whistle, etc.). My advice is to work out a very general schedule built primarily around nap times, which accustoms the child to sleeping at a particular time and saves a lot of arguing and whining.

Number Two: Food

Did you know that babies should have whole milk up to the age of two, rather than 2 percent, because fat is necessary for their brains? I didn't, and I'm a home economist, so my guess is that other grandmothers don't know either.

It is up to parents to educate themselves and to know what their child should and should not eat. If you explain why your baby should be eating this and shouldn't be eating that, there is no Granny-Nanny in the world who will disagree, especially if you cite a pediatrician. No fruit juice, says the dentist? No fruit juice, says the Granny-Nanny.

The allergenic qualities of peanuts weren't widely known until a decade or so ago. So if Mother says no peanut butter, Granny-Nanny should agree. And if Mother says some other food is causing diarrhea or whatever, again Granny-Nanny should eliminate it from menus. On the other hand, if the Granny-Nanny sees a reaction to some particular food, Mother needs to pay attention. There is a very good possibility that from the grandmother's experience she knows what she is talking about.

One of the problems that is bound to come up is the "I don't like it" syndrome. This can be troubling to a grandparent who has taken the time to make that particular dish and fully believes it is good for the child. Should the complaint be ignored, which might be encouraging bad behavior? Or should a child be forced to sit there until he's eaten or at least tasted the dish? This is up to the mother, not the Granny-Nanny, no matter how much work has gone into the preparation of the dish. And Granny-Nanny shouldn't take it personally. Perhaps the child's body is signaling that it is allergic to a particular food. Or it may simply be that his or her taste buds have not yet developed for that particular food. Or it may be a power trip on the part of the child. Remember all the foods—onions and pickles and ripe olives—that you didn't like as a child, and that you now absolutely love. (Well, at least tolerate.)

What about a child who doesn't eat at all . . . or who doesn't clean his plate? Since the chances are that the child will eat most of his meals at his own home or with his parents, it's their call. Do they send the child away from the table? Do they put the plate in the refrigerator and heat it up later when the child is hungry? Whatever they do, so should you.

All other things being equal, one has to take the grandchild's likes and dislikes into account. If she rejects oatmeal and loves Cheerios, then by all means, she should be served Cheerios. On the other hand, if she requires special foods for medical reasons, the parents should provide them and the grandparents should serve them. Parents who want their child to eat organic foods, which are expensive and not always easy to find locally, should provide them to the Granny-Nanny.

In all of these matters, on which there are numerous potential disagreements, remember one thing—both parents and Granny-Nanny have the well-being of the child as the primary concern.

Number Three: Television

Specifically, how much of it and what kind of shows. The former may depend on the weather, the latter should be determined by the parent. (Can you believe that more than three decades ago *Mr. Rogers' Neighborhood* was a popular choice for youngsters and, despite his passing, is still going strong? I confess I didn't appreciate the calming qualities of Mr. Rogers until now, when I see my grandchildren react to him. As for *Sesame Street*, it has been teaching kids numbers and letters since 1968.)

To avoid plopping the kids in front of the TV on a rainy day (but don't say it that way), suggest alternate activities (see Appendix 1, page 188 for ideas). The most common one? Go to any mall on a rainy day and see the parade of grand-parents pushing their grandchildren in strollers.

It is an amazing fact that parents whose TV sets are on from morning till night will object to the Granny-Nanny doing the same. An obvious case of do as I say, not as I do.

Then there's the books-versus-television contention. One mother allowed as how she'd much rather have Granny-Nanny read a book than turn on a DVD. Fortunately for all concerned, there is an alternative—the Scholastic collection of DVDs that animate favorite children's books. And they have an unusual effect on some children. After watching the DVD, many kids want to read the book. I suspect it is because the DVD goes by too quickly, while the child can set his own pace while reading the book. There is also the recognition factor—look, there's the fox hiding in the haystack in *Rosie's Walk* by Pat Hutchins (Aladdin; 1971), or see, over there, the banana in *Good Night, Gorilla* by Peggy Rathmann (G. P. Putnam's Sons; board edition, 1996).

Number Four: Blinkies, Hoppies, And Thumbs

Many children find security in carrying around a blinkie (or blankie, actually a blanket) or a Hoppy (soft, droopy toy). That was a no-no decades ago. "Experts" believed it destroyed a child's self-confidence to depend on exterior things. All that's changed. Today, according to Wendy Goldband Schunick (author of *Tooth Fairy Tales*), writing in *Baby and Nursery Magazine*, "Most child experts advocate the use of a comfort item. Babies naturally begin to bond to a blanket or stuffed animal, regardless of the parents' unique parenting style. It is important to note that attachment to a lovey is not a sign that a child has not been nurtured by her parents or that they have not bonded. Actually, the opposite is true. Parents who respond to a baby's needs for assurance will instill confidence and self-esteem in their little one. It is this inner strength that will give the child confidence to slowly learn the needed skill of self-comfort."

So, if the mother has provided the blanket/toy, and the children are in their own home, Granny-Nanny should keep her mouth shut. If the children are at Grandma's, the parents should provide duplicates to be kept there. It is such a small thing in an adult's world and such a large thing in a child's world—this is an area for concession. I have known college kids to take a favorite stuffed animal with them to their dorm room. So long as they don't carry it around with them on campus, what's the big deal?

Thumb-sucking traditionally has been discouraged on the basis of damage to the children's teeth or, more accurately, the child's bite—we're talking braces here. However, recent studies note that while about 50 percent of one-year-old infants suck their thumb, most children stop by the age of four or five years. Only about 15 to 20 percent of six-year-old children persist in the habit. Even then, the sucking is not continuous during the day and stops once the child falls asleep. As one mother noted, "Having had four children (three of them thumb-suckers) I can tell you not one of them went off to college with this habit . . . also, it was the non-thumb-sucker who needed braces."

If you have a children's dentist, and he agrees with you that thumb-sucking is not as pernicious as has been generally thought, cite him as an authority when discussing it with Granny-Nanny. But, if you want to discourage thumb-sucking, there are more than a dozen clever children's books to help you persuade Granny and the little sucker to give up the habit.

Is The Cure Worse Than The Habit?

I personally think some of the proposed cures—rubbing garlic, lemon juice, and, of all things, Tabasco on the thumb—are almost worse than the habit. However, not quite so bad as the cure used by one family who lived on a farm: they went out to the chicken house to find the stuff to rub on a thumb. Now, that was gross!

Number Five: Routines

Habits and traditions are very important to children; they are comforting. If the habits don't endanger a child's health and well-being, and if they don't actually drive adults around the bend, they can go a long way toward helping maintain a child's good humor. It's important for parents to alert Granny-Nannies about any special habits their children have and to enlist the grandparents' cooperation. For example, if a child likes to go barefoot inside the house, provide slippers. If the child likes to take the slippers off, you should let the Granny-Nanny know so she can make sure to sweep and vacuum thoroughly. If a child likes to sleep without a pillow, pillows should be removed from the bed because they're just going to end up on the floor anyway.

Wait a minute, you say. Haven't I forgotten something? The number-one issue in childrearing? Not at all. I'll get to it in a minute (translated as a couple of pages).

Words To Live By
(You might want to post these on your refrigerator)

1. If it's the best solution, accept the challenge gracefully and do the very best you can.

2. Lavish the grandchildren with positive feedback on everything from play habits to first drawings to schoolwork. Your praise will help them build the self-esteem they'll need to get along in the world.

3. Be sympathetic and supportive when the parents are tired, discouraged, or having parenting difficulties.

4. Resist the temptation to intervene with advice and criticism, even though you feel your experience is greater.

---

5. Live by the rules set by the parents. The children are theirs, not yours. If you really feel strongly about a particular point, let the pediatrician make the decision.

6. Be careful about the things you do and say . . . There's a good chance they'll be parroted from your home to their home. The only name-calling a child should hear is that of his given name.

7. Make a safe environment for the little ones; it will be easier on both you and them.

8. Take as much enjoyment from it as you can. It will be over before you know it.

9. Do not be quick to tell a new mother about each new milestone her child achieves. You do want to share the accomplishments of the day, but be judicious about it. Realize that in your desire to tell all, you may make her feel guilty for not being there to see the first crawl or the first step, or hear that first word. She may say she appreciates it, but the disappointment on her face says something else.

10. Enough is enough! As a rule of thumb, if you're under fifty-five, you can handle three children . . . two if you're under sixty-five. And if you're over sixty-five, one's a lot. Over seventy, no matter the number, you need help!

And remember the golden rule of grandparenthood: Love 'em, spoil 'em, and send 'em home! Guess what? You'll get a chance to do the same thing all over again tomorrow.

CHAPTER 16

"He Said, She Said"

Honest disagreement is often
a good sign of progress.

—Gandhi

By now you should have worked out a lot of decisions, such as where Granny-Nanny will care for the kids, what she'll be paid or not, her hours, the children's TV time, and so much more.

It is now time to put pen to paper. No, I am not talking about a contract, although with an actual nanny you'd have her sign an actual contract. But neither parent nor grandparent is planning to sue the other in the event the agreement unravels. So, "no contract," say I under the advice of counsel, in this case Margaret Phiambolis, Esq., a labor lawyer.

What I am suggesting is that you put your agreements in writing so that everyone knows where things stand. It also can help clarify decisions that have been made . . . and decisions yet to be made . . . as in any business situation.

For Example, Vacations

Who gets to choose vacation times? Hadn't thought of that, had you? If the Granny-Nanny couple is retired, it's probably not a problem. They can tailor their schedule to the parents' easily. If one grandparent still works, how many weeks of vacation does she get compared to the parents? As a suggestion, you might want to alternate years (one year the grandparents choose first and the next, the parents do). But the deciding factor has to be the parents' work schedule.

Why? Because when the parents go on vacation, the grandparents automatically are freed of their duties . . . unless. No. That wouldn't happen, would it? That the parents go away and leave the children with the grandparents? It might, under certain circumstances. So put that in the agreement. If the parents want to use their vacation time to extend maternity leave, they can make that decision nine months in advance and should discuss it with the Granny-Nanny nine months in advance.

You can see how many things there are to think about in advance and, hopefully, agree upon as well.

Based on my own experiences and interviews with others, I have prepared a sample checklist (see below). Use it, abuse it, ignore it, but at least it is a starting point. When it comes to discipline, I've listed five possibilities on page 128. There may be more. It's up to you, but for now I'd leave numbers 6 through 10 blank, since this is something that we haven't discussed yet. My feeling is: climb the little hills before you tackle the mountain.

Also, no need to be formal and sign anything. You all know (both parents and the Granny-Nanny) what you've agreed to. Initial if it makes you feel better.

Sample Parent/Granny-Nanny Checklist

•Where will the Granny-Nannying take place? _____

•If childproofing is necessary, who will pay for it? _____ What will it consist of ?_____

•What percentage of the furniture, equipment, and toys necessary to care for the child/children in the Granny-Nanny's home will be the parents' responsibility?

_____

•How many meals will the Granny-Nanny be responsible for? _____

•Who will pay for this food or will it be divided up in some way, such as baby foods provided by parents, regular foods by Granny-Nanny? _____

_____

•Transportation costs for necessary trips via _____ (mode) will be paid for by _____

•Other costs, such as X, Y, and Z, will be covered by _____

•Will there be a salary? _____ How much will it be? _____
When will it be paid: daily, weekly, bimonthly, or monthly? _____

•If the number of children increases, will the payment increase? _____
If so, by how much? _____

•What will the hours be? _____

•If the parents run late or if there is an overnight, will that affect the payment?
_____ If so, by how much? _____

•How will vacations be decided? _____ Must they be taken at
one time or can they be split up? _____

•Will sick days be available? _____ If so, how many?_____
Will they be paid for?_____

•Will mother supply a daily schedule? _____ Will Granny-Nanny abide
by it?_____ Under what conditions will compromises be made?
_____

•Blinkies, OK?_____ Hoppies?_____ Thumb-sucking?_____
Pacifiers?_____ Teething rings?_____

•How much TV time as a general rule? _____

•Under what circumstances should the Granny-Nanny call the mother? _____
_____. And what phone number should she use?
_____

•If either party wishes to end the relationship, how much notice would be fair?
_____

Discipline
(To be filled in later—here are a few possibilities)

Which, if any, of the following forms of discipline are acceptable to both parents and grandparents?

1. Time-out_____

2. Standing in corner_____

3. Deprivation of desired object_____

4. Being sent to bedroom_____

5. Hand-slapping_____

6. _____

7. _____

8. _____

9. _____

10. _____

PART V

Controversy

When a thing ceases to be a subject of controversy,
it ceases to be a subject of interest.

—William Hazlitt

CHAPTER 17

Discipline

It takes tremendous discipline
to control the influence, the power you have
over other people's lives.

—Clint Eastwood

The day I find myself quoting a movie actor!! But it's true, especially in the context of grandparents, parents, and kids. After all, who has more power than adults over children? Unfortunately, some adults use it more than others, and some use it badly. Others do things just right and end up with children who are not cowed and who are capable of great feats of self-discipline.

First, some definitions: according to the American Heritage Dictionary of the English Language, Fourth Edition, the verbs "to discipline" and "to punish" are defined as follows:

Discipline (v.)

1. To train by instruction and practice, especially to teach self-control to.

2. To teach to obey rules or accept authority.

Punish (v.)

1. To subject to a penalty for an offense, sin, or fault.

2. To inflict a penalty for (an offense).

3. To handle roughly; hurt.

I find it interesting that these two words are at once so similar and so different. The meanings of each seem to pass through an invisible barrier, and, on the other side, the words meld into each other, depending on the context in which they are used or understood.

Spanking

Before we begin, let's make sure we know what we are talking about. Spanking is not swatting and vice versa.

To swat: to strike once with the flat of the hand on a well-padded behind. Literally, it should be a case of "this hurts me more than it does you."

To spank: to strike repeatedly with either the hand or an instrument on a behind that may or may not be padded. The intention is to inflict pain.

In the interest of complete disclosure, I should declare my own point of view as well. I am against spanking. And I realize I am in a minority. A 1994 survey at the Albert Einstein College of Medicine in New York found that 74 percent of parents believed it was appropriate to spank children between the ages of one and three, while 19 percent approved of spanking children under the age of one. A 1995 Harris Poll found that 80 percent of parents surveyed had spanked their children, while 87 percent said spanking is sometimes appropriate. These numbers are declining. In 1968, 94 percent of the adult population believed it was sometimes necessary to spank.

Whether we agree with this or not, the point here is that it is parents who are cited throughout this study and others as well. Not Granny-Nannies. Spanking is the parents' prerogative; it is not within the Granny-Nanny's province. Let me repeat that: SPANKING IS NOT WITHIN THE GRANNY-NANNY'S PROVINCE.

Our obligation, like that of the physician, is to do no harm. Spanking can harm—emotionally and physically. For example, Jan Hunt, M.Sc., reports that "blows to the lower end of the spinal column send shock waves along the length of the spine, and may injure the child. . . . Some children have become paralyzed through nerve damage from spanking, and some have died after mild paddlings, due to undiagnosed medical complications."

According to family therapists it is possible that a parent or adult intending to discipline a child may actually abuse or punish that child instead. The majority of child welfare investigations that substantiate emotional or physical abuse of children involve parents who are attempting to discipline, rather than abuse, their children. But more on that later.

Spanking: Discipline Or Punishment?

Discipline is frequently confused with punishment. There are people who believe that spanking their children is a form of discipline, not punishment.

According to the American Academy of Pediatrics, **spanking is the least effective way to discipline** (their emphasis, and mine, too).

However, even the Academy believes that there are times when a spanking seems reasonable. The example they cite is that of a child running out into the street.

A parent or caregiver will run after the child, swoop her up, and bring her to safety, and then, almost without thinking, will spank the child to communicate and emphasize the sharp sense of anxiety for the child's well-being that the adult is experiencing.

The question is: What does the Academy—and what do you, and I—consider a spanking in this case? A swat on the rear? Bending her over your knee and whaling the tar out of her? A hard blow to the handiest spot available, her face or head? It does make a difference.

Spanking a child is a controversial matter. The social customs and laws concerning corporal punishment vary greatly from region to region and country to country. Many people believe that corporal punishment is violent and abusive and should be outlawed in modern society. Others say spanking can be administered in acceptable forms as a disciplinary measure.

Two proponents of disciplinary spanking are Den A. Trumbull, M.D., and S. DuBose Ravenel, M.D. In their essay, "Spare the Rod?" (published in *Family Policy* by the Family Research Council, 1996), they wrote, "The critical issue is how spanking is used more so than whether or not it is used. Physical abuse by an angry, uncontrolled parent (or caregiver) will leave lasting emotional wounds and cultivate bitterness and resentment within a child. The balanced, prudent use of disciplinary spanking, however, is an effective deterrent to aggressive behavior with some children."

Almost everyone seems to agree that spanking with an implement is not acceptable. Such punishment can cause bruises, welts, swellings, and hematomas and burst blood vessels in the lungs or brain. These embolisms can even be fatal. Striking with a heavy or hard implement can also easily fracture the tail-bone (coccyx).

According to traditional psychology, there is a cause–effect relationship between traumatic childhood events and adult sexual deviation, drug and alcohol abuse, and emotional problems. Perhaps the best advice is to go very light on corporal punishment, or perhaps use none at all, and balance it with lots of praise and hugs for good behavior.

Maintaining the fine line between a swat for a minor offense and blows on the behind with a strap for something of a more grievous nature can be difficult in certain situations. **But it is not your decision to make, not your line to maintain.** Your first line of defense against such actions is to remember that **these are not your children.** A Granny-Nanny should have a clear understanding with the parents of what they believe are acceptable disciplinary measures to use with their children—whether a gentle slap, confinement to a corner, no TV privileges, or absolutely no acts of punishment at all.

Soap? Nope!

Another controversial method of "discipline" is washing a child's mouth out with soap, used as a means to discourage talking back, bad words, biting, and other acts that children use to test adults. Judging from mothers I've consulted, this practice of grinding a bar of soap in a child's mouth appears to be quite common. **Once again, this is something parents may choose to do, but grandparents never.**

Why so? Because as one mother pointed out to me, "Soap isn't edible, nor can it be used as a replacement for air. A crying child will heave, gasp, and hiccup. One of these days you will discover your child convulsing, choking, vomiting, or having a severe allergic reaction to something in the soap, or the child could die from soap inhalation. You can't simply tell your child to stop breathing for a few minutes. That's deprivation of oxygen to their brains."

The Secret Of Effective Discipline

That secret is the ability to create a consequence for children that enables them to learn and understand the lesson. Example: showing a child that a lightbulb is hot and can burn. One doesn't actually have to burn the child, just hold a hand near the bulb and say, "Hot!" Child care professionals say this kind of learning consequence is far more effective than physical consequences such as spanking, slapping, washing the mouth out with soap . . . or verbal consequences such as scolding, belittling, and the silent treatment.

If you force a child to do something against his will (especially by physically overpowering him) he will soon develop a sense of helplessness and victimization (and you may even turn him into a victimizer himself). Being bigger doesn't give you permission to bully or belittle.

Spanked children may feel unloved by their parents or caregivers. They may feel that they can't cope and can't meet adults' high expectations. Spanked children may become shy and withdrawn, or an opposite behavior pattern may occur. In the latter, the child stores up negative emotions and releases them in angry outbursts, temper tantrums, and other aggressive behavior, such as bullying siblings and classmates.

On the other hand, time-outs, restrictions, removal of toys, "Dennis the Menace" sitting in the corner (or standing, as the case may be)—these are all forms of discipline that might be used by a Granny-Nanny and therefore need to be discussed in advance and agreed upon.

Practical Responses You Can Live With

I wish there were a chart one could consult that would list various offenses and offer possible effective responses. There isn't. Nor would one work. **Discipline should take place at the time of the offense,** not after one has gone to consult a chart. A delay in disciplining a child has two effects: if the child is young, he may not remember clearly what he did to cause the discipline. If the child is older and knows something is coming, he may try to avoid it by hiding, which just makes the whole situation worse.

However, For What It Is Worth, Here Are A Few Tricks For Granny-Nannies To Use:

• **Give hugs and kisses a try**. Especially with the child who is out of control. The physical act of hugging gives you physical control of the child. The kissing makes it seem less of a physical contest.

• **A screaming contest**, or I can scream louder than you!

• **Diversion:** You're scaring the cat!

• **"Igg-a-Nore."** A very effective code word meaning to ignore the behavior when the act is a cry for attention. (We also use the code words: "Eeyore's first cousin." For those who don't remember, Eeyore is the sad donkey in *Winnie-the-Pooh*.)

• Because I sometimes walk with a cane, I **threaten to "hook them."** They're half-scared, half-tempted. What would hooking with my cane be like? If I can help it, they'll never find out.

• **The countdown**... or should I say count up... to what, the child doesn't know but imagines it will be something awful. (Do not announce how high you are going to count, otherwise at the magic number, you have to deliver.)

• **Stare them down:** Get down to eye level and warn them that trouble is coming.

• **Or tower over them** so that they have to bend their heads way back to look at you. It emphasizes their helplessness.

• **When something is thrown, it has been bad and has to go away for a while.** Never pretend to throw something out and not do it. Children are quick to detect a fake.

• Finally, remember you are an adult. **Adults were born to outsmart kids.**

Sibling Rivalry

If your sister hits you, don't hit her back. They always catch the second person.

—Elaine Shelton

It's one of the most common and most difficult situations to handle. And in some cases, the only thing that works is separating the children for long periods of time, as for example sending them to different schools.

Here, the parents and Granny-Nanny must work in concert. It's called a united front and is an absolute necessity.

In fact, you should work out together what should be done if one child is in the habit of doing something to the other. For example, if one child pulls the hair of another, do you pull the offending child's hair, or do you use a time-out? If one bites the other, do you bite, too (but not to make a mark), or do you put the offender in a corner? Trickier still, what if a child throws things at Granny-Nanny? I am not in favor of throwing back, but deprivation of the toy does seem in order.

It is certainly a Granny-Nanny's right to ask in advance how she should handle siblings who fight. This happens a lot, and the resolution should be agreed upon.

In any event, it is a nice touch if all can agree that the final resolution of the problem must be hugs all around and an apology.

CHAPTER 18

Abuse

Synonyms: *abuse, misuse, mistreat, ill-treat, maltreat*

These verbs mean to treat wrongfully or harmfully. Abuse applies to injurious or improper treatment.

—The American Heritage Dictionary
of the English Language, Fourth Edition

These are my definitions of **abuse**, **neglect**, and **threatened harm**, especially as they relate to children and parents/caregivers:

Abuse (n): Nonaccidental, that is, deliberate, infliction of physical or psychological injury or sexual abuse by a parent, adult household member, or other person responsible for care of the child.

Neglect (n): Failure/omission by a caregiver to provide the care, supervision, services, or protection necessary to maintain physical and mental health.

Threatened Harm (phrase): Circumstances, physical evidence, or behavior that leads a prudent person to have reasonable cause to suspect abuse or neglect has occurred or may occur in the immediate future if no intervention is provided.

The Prevalence Of Child Abuse

On June 25, 2003, Congress mandated that the Department of Health and Human Services (DHHS) conduct, in 2005, the fourth national survey of incidence of maltreatment of children. If this National Incidence Survey (NIS-4) holds true to form, the results will be horrifying. These are the results of the three previous surveys:

• In 1980, NIS-1 estimated that 625,000 children were abused or neglected per year.

• In 1986, NIS-2 estimated a total of 931,000 abused or neglected children.

• In 1993, NIS-3 estimated a total of 1,553,800 abused or neglected children per year, **a 67 percent increase over the 1986 estimate and a 149 percent increase over the 1980 estimate.**

What Do We Know About These Children?

According to the DHHS report:

• Girls are sexually abused three times more often than boys.

• Boys have a greater risk of emotional neglect and of serious injury than girls.

• Children are consistently vulnerable to sexual abuse from age three on.

There were no significant racial differences in the incidence of maltreatment or maltreatment-related injuries uncovered in either the NIS-2 or the NIS-3.

Family Characteristics

• Children of single parents had a 77 percent greater risk of being harmed by physical abuse, an 87 percent greater risk of being harmed by physical neglect, and an 80 percent greater risk of suffering serious injury or harm from abuse or neglect than children living with both parents.

• Children in the largest families were physically neglected at nearly three times the rate of those who came from single-child families.

• Children from families with annual incomes below $15,000 as compared to children from families with annual incomes above $30,000 per year were over twenty-two times more likely to experience some form of maltreatment that fit the "harm standard" (i.e., they had already experienced harm from abuse or neglect) and over twenty-five times more likely to suffer some form of maltreatment as defined by the "endangerment standard," which is less stringent.

• Children from the lowest-income families were eighteen times more likely to be sexually abused, almost fifty-six times more likely to be educationally neglected, and over twenty-two times more likely to be seriously injured from maltreatment as defined under the harm standard than children from the higher-income families.

If a million and a half cases are reported, how many go unreported?

Officials estimate that **fewer than 30 percent of child abuse cases are reported, and of those, fewer than 30 percent will be investigated by child protective services.** Which, if my math is correct, means that **90 percent of all incidences go unreported or uninvestigated.**

The Family Factor

Even more shocking, four out of five reports of child abuse to police involve family members. Not pedophiles, kidnappers, gangs, druggies, or pornographers. Not foster parents, teachers, hired caregivers, neighbors, or friends. **Blood relations!**

Caregivers And Abuse

Is child abuse a real concern among parents whose young children are under the supervision of caregivers? Sixty percent of parents surveyed by one national child care organization said they were "very concerned" that their children could experience abuse or neglect in a day care center. This concern exists despite federal statistics indicating that fewer than 2 percent of reported cases of abuse are perpetrated by faculty, staff, or nonrelative child care providers. The National Committee to Prevent Child Abuse puts the figure for out-of-home child care abuse only slightly higher at 3 percent.

Admittedly the majority of those family members causing child abuse are the parents. The rest are siblings and close relatives, and yes, grandparents.

Two Thoughts On Grandparents And Abuse

1. One of the parents knows if the grandparents showed any tendencies toward abuse when he or she was being reared.

2. Any grandparents considering Granny-Nannying must look long and hard at themselves and consider the possibility that child abuse could occur on their watch.

Knowing how grandparents raised their own children shouldn't be the only criterion for setting up Granny-Nanny care. People change with age. A mild, loving parent may have morphed into an irate, fast-to-anger senior citizen.

Best Advice For Parents

1. Observe how the grandparents treat your children when visiting your home or when hosting your family.

2. Check the medications that potential Granny-Nannies are taking. Some of their pharmaceuticals may be causing mood swings or worse.

3. Talk to Granny-Nanny's family doctor. Ask if the grandparents are physically and mentally up to being "parents" again.

4. Have a heart-to-heart discussion with your prospective Granny-Nanny about child abuse. It's a delicate matter but needs to be aired.

Best Advice For Granny-Nanny

Suppose the shoe is on the other foot and you, the Granny-Nanny, observe child abuse or neglect in the parents' home. It is obligatory that the Granny-Nanny step in. Getting the children into your own care for a few hours a day can reduce the opportunities for child abuse. It can also relieve a lot of pressure on young parents who may simply be too tired or stressed out to properly care for their infants.

But if you continue to suspect abuse, what then? You have to do something about it. (Real abuse is one thing, suspected is another. Making wild accusations can get you and the parents into legal trouble.) If you suspect abuse, the most effective thing you can do is warn the parents that you are prepared to take further steps if it continues.

Tell them you have no choice, that reporting abuse is mandatory in all fifty states. You don't have to tell them that it's mandatory just for professionals except in those eighteen states where "any person" is required to report it.

Verbal Abuse

It is a fact that verbal abuse can be as damaging to a child as physical blows. Constant berating, demeaning criticisms, and threats are no-nos. Calm, patient explanations of wrong-doings and why they are wrong and what to do next time are helpful to children in their learning and behavioral patterning.

Bruises

It's a good idea to do a bruise check when the child arrives for Granny-Nannying and just before departure. That way both you and the parents will know when something occurred, and there will be no unfounded recriminations. Discussing boo-boos with the child can also be helpful in determining their cause and give you clues on how to eliminate danger points in the home. Verbally and visually identifying areas dangerous to the child can be very effective. Try saying the word *Danger!* whenever a child approaches a forbidden area. It works.

"Force Feeding"

A lesser, but nonetheless frequent, form of child abuse is forcing the child to do something he or she doesn't want to do. For example, the child won't eat a certain food. As I noted before, the familiar "I don't like it" can be troubling to a grandparent who has taken the time to make that particular dish and who fully believes it is good for the child. Forcing the food on a child can be frustrating and messy, to say nothing of fostering stubborn traits and moody behavior.

Consider that the child's body may be signaling that it's allergic to that particular food. Or it may simply be that his or her taste buds have not yet developed for that particular food.

An Exception To Every Rule

Another example of abuse can be too strict an enforcement of rules. It may be nice for you, and Mommy may have dictated that the child is supposed to nap every day at 2 P.M., but many factors determine whether the child is ready to nap at that time on any given day. These factors include extra sleep the night before, excitement of any kind, illness, and a desire to finish something already under way, whether it's a TV program or a play activity.

If the child isn't tired, he isn't tired. And locking him in his bedroom is not the answer. (Not that it leads to homosexuality or a tendency to masturbate—that is a myth from Grandmother's childhood.) Skipping a nap won't kill him, he'll just want to go to bed earlier that night. What may happen, however, is that a nonsleepy bored child, unobserved in his bedroom, can find all sorts of things to disassemble or experiment with. Ballpoint pens stuck into electric outlets mean trouble.

A little flexibility will go a long way toward avoiding hassles and not upsetting the child. Find ways to make taking a nap fun. More than one Granny-Nanny has resorted to saying, "Pooh Bear (or Miss Mousy or Tinky Winky or Blue) is really tired and wants to take a nap with you." Reading a bedtime story helps, as does turning off the TV and playing some soothing music.

I have a confession to make: to get my four-year-old granddaughter to use the potty before nap time, she and I have pee-pee races. Whoever tinkles first wins. She beats me every time and is off to bed crowing loudly. And I don't mind a bit since that means not having to do a load of laundry every night.

Crying Jags, Or That's A Whale Of A Wail

Long wailing sessions are hard on everyone's nerves. In fact, they are very often the trigger that leads to abuse. A slap to the face to stop the wailing brings on more crying, which results in a harder slap, which well, you get the picture.

So, how do you stop the wailing? Gags? Abusive. Soap? Abusive. Cookies? Does that reward crying? Tough call—and one that has to be worked out between parents and grandparents.

Perceived Violence

Still another form of child abuse is allowing the child to see violence committed between parents, grandparents, siblings, or others. **Abuse is violence, and violence walks down the generational ladder. Children learn from their parents and from caregivers.** If children under your care witness or experience abuse on a regular basis, they are more likely to bring the same conditions to their own partnering and parenting in later life. Suspend any differences you have between you and your spouse (or you and the parents), petty or volcanic, until after the kids have left for the day.

How Can You Tell If A Child Has Been Abused?

I personally have never seen abuse, but the folks at The BabyCenter (www.baby-center.com) suggest the following:

Keep an eye out for physical symptoms and behavioral changes that may point to abuse, although it can be tricky to figure out exactly what's going on. "You're always playing a guessing game," says Kathy Baxter, director of the San Francisco Child Abuse Council. "A child could have many other reasons for acting out, being fussy, or becoming withdrawn. But parents are really good at knowing their children, so you have to try to put together a picture and go with your gut instinct."

If your child is old enough to talk, Baxter suggests regularly asking him questions, such as, "Did anything happen to you today that you didn't like?" or "Have you ever been frightened at day care [or Granny's]?" If he's in the habit of telling you what makes him uncomfortable, he'll be more likely to tell you if anything is seriously amiss. "When it comes to abuse and neglect, most kids tell the truth," Baxter says. "But in most cases, they are reluctant. They don't want to get the person in trouble. They feel guilty; they feel it happened because they were bad."

If your toddler isn't talking well enough to tell you what's going on, pinpointing abuse can be even more difficult. What you can do is keep a close eye on your child for signs that all is not well. Some parents discover signs of abuse—such as internal bleeding and injuries—only when they take their child to a pediatrician because he won't stop crying or is excessively fussy.

What Should You Look For In An Abused Child?

A Child Who Has Been *Physically* Abused May:

• Cry and put up a fight when it's time to go to day care, or appear frightened around the caregiver or other adults.

• Come home with unexplained bruises, abrasions, burns, broken bones, black eyes, cuts, bite marks, or other injuries. ***Repeated injuries of any type can be a warning sign.***

A Child Who Has Been *Emotionally* Abused May:

• Display behavioral problems or changes such as shunning a parent's affections —or, alternately, becoming excessively clingy—or acting angry or depressed. Abused children often show extremes in behavior: A normally outgoing and assertive child may become unusually compliant and passive, while a generally mild child may act in a demanding and aggressive manner.

• Become less talkative or stop communicating almost completely, or may display signs of a speech disorder such as stuttering.

• Act inappropriately adult or infantile. For example, a toddler may either become overly protective and "parental" toward other children, or revert to rocking and head banging

• Be delayed physically or emotionally, walking or talking later than expected or continuing to have regular temper tantrums. But since every child develops at a different rate, it can be difficult to determine whether a developmental delay stems from abuse.

• Complain of headaches or stomachaches that have no medical cause.

A Child Who Has Been *Sexually* Abused May:

• Have pain, itching, bleeding, or bruises in or around the genital area.

• Have difficulty walking or sitting, possibly because of genital or anal pain.

• Suffer from urinary tract infections, or suddenly start wetting the bed.

• Be reluctant to take off his coat or sweater, even on a hot day, or insist on wearing multiple undergarments.

• Demonstrate sexual knowledge, curiosity, or behavior beyond his age (obsessive curiosity about sexual matters, for example, or seductive behavior toward peers or adults).

For heaven's sake, if you see violence or abuse in the child's life, do something about it. Even though one of the abusers is your own flesh and blood, take remedial action. Call the police in the most aggravated circumstances. Talk to a women's aid organization or social services. The federal DHHS, Children's Bureau, has published a "how to" site including hotline phone numbers for most states, "***How to Report Suspected Abuse and Neglect***." Remember, not all numbers are manned twenty-four/seven. For more information:

www.acf.dhhs.gov/programs/cb/publications/rpt_abu.htm

The USA National Hotline is 1-800-4-A-CHILD (1-800-422-4453).

Child Care Resources On Child Abuse
(For Granny-Nanny And/Or Parents)

National Clearinghouse on Child Abuse and Neglect Information
http://nccanch.acf.hhs.gov

National Network for Child Care
www.nncc.org

National Association of Child Care Resources and Referral Agencies
www.naccrra.org

National Committee to Prevent Child Abuse
www.childabuse.org

CHAPTER 19

A Quiz

It is better to know some of the questions
than all of the answers.

—James Thurber

This is the shortest chapter in the book,
yet one that may take the most thinking.
These questions were culled from final exams
for child development courses.

How Would You Handle The Following Situations?
(There are no right or wrong answers.)

1. A child punctures a king-size waterbed that holds enough water to fill a 2,000-square-foot house four inches deep.

2. A three-year-old child raises her voice in a restaurant and drowns out two hundred adults.

3. Someone manages to hook a dog leash over a ceiling fan that is not strong enough to rotate a forty-two-pound boy wearing Batman underwear and a Superman cape.

4. A ceiling fan is being used as a baseball bat. Of course, it takes a few throws until ball hits bat/fan, which is running. Even double-pane glass won't stop a baseball hit by a ceiling fan.

5. You hear the toilet flush and the words "oh, oh"!

6. You discover that a six-year-old can start a fire with a flint rock even though a sixty-six-year-old man says it only happens in the movies.

7. You discover that certain Legos are missing from the group your four-year-old was playing with. (I have it on good authority that certain Legos will pass through the digestive tract of a four-year-old.)

8. A little girl tries to cook her Play-Doh apple pie in your microwave.

9. You get living proof that super glue is forever.

10. You attempt to insert a videotape into a VCR only to discover a peanut butter and jelly sandwich got there first. Despite the TV commercials showing the contrary, the eject button doesn't work.

11. To the sound of a bloodcurdling cry, you find out that even superstrong garbage bags do not make good parachutes.

12. Father comes in from mowing the grass to announce that marbles in the machine's gas tank make a lot of noise when mowing.

13. You remind yourself—again—to always check the oven for plastic toys before turning the oven on.

And finally, since thirteen is bad luck:

14. You hear a horrendous screech from the dryer. You open the door and a cat jumps out. Although earthworms do not get dizzy or dry out in a dryer, cats do. Cats throw up twice their body weight when sick.

PART VI

Making The Best Of It

It is very strange that the years teach us patience—that the shorter our time, the greater our capacity for waiting.

—Elizabeth Taylor

You can learn many things from children. How much patience you have, for instance.

—Franklin P. Jones

Patience is one virtue which will come in handy as we face the difficulties, crises, and heartbreak that may arise in the lives of our children and grandchildren.

CHAPTER 20

The Special Child

Each child comes into the world with unique potential.
The biggest challenge for parents and teachers is to
remove the roadblocks that keep those gifts from being
recognized, celebrated, and nurtured.

—Thomas Armstrong, psychologist and educator

Here's What The Numbers Say . . .

Until recently, no one knew officially how many preschool children had disabilities. Although there had been surveys taken and estimates made, no one had bothered to ask in previous censuses. Finally, in 2000, they did ask—and the results were staggering.

One of every twelve U.S. children and teenagers—5.2 million in all—had a physical or mental disability. Based on other studies, this reflected sharp growth in the nation's young disabled population over the previous decade. The disabilities captured by the census ranged in severity from mild asthma to serious mental illness or mental retardation demanding full-time care.

The figures, which covered children ages five to twenty, are the first ever collected on childhood disability in the decennial census in more than a century. But data from other sources have shown a rapid increase in the number and rate of childhood disabilities.

Special needs now are generally understood to include mild mental retardation, autism, cerebral palsy, AIDS, blindness, deafness, and physical disabilities. Special care, which can often be provided by Granny-Nanny, is also required for children with asthma, severe allergies, and emotional problems.

Special education enrollment rose twice as fast as overall school enrollment in the 1990s and by 2000 represented more than 10 percent of public school children. Learning difficulties, which have been recognized as a disability for twenty years or so, account for about half of these special children.

The research on the subject indicates that early intervention seems to help children with developmental disabilities advance closer to the norm for their age group. Most of the research that has been done to date was conducted in the U.S., but a great deal is now being conducted internationally. There are now all sorts of journals devoted exclusively to the subject, such as *Exceptional Children*,

Remedial and Special Education, *Learning Disabilities Quarterly*, *Journal of Learning Disabilities*, and *Learning Disabilities Research and Practice*.

A Precious Gift

There is little that a Granny-Nanny can do that is as valuable and, sometimes, as difficult as caring for a child with special needs. Only a parent, whose time may be limited because of work, is as well qualified to give the love and devotion required.

Overwhelmingly, the research shows that grandparents can and do provide a lot of support for children with disabilities. However, to be honest, many grandparents find it difficult to accept the child's disability and thus tend to be less supportive, which is as one might expect. For most of his or her life, Granny-Nanny may have had little contact with children with disabilities. In the past, many such children were cared for away from home or even hidden away in institutions. Mainstreaming of the disadvantaged in a school? Not on your life! It was a cockamamie dream thirty, forty years ago.

Not any longer. Society's acceptance of children with disabilities has changed, and for the better. The move toward inclusion, or mainstreaming, of children with disabilities in schools and activities is also fostering more in-family care and integration into regular family life. The child with special needs is no longer thought of as an oddity.

It hasn't hurt that many well-known people—some of them noted intellectuals, such as Albert Einstein and Woodrow Wilson (who didn't read until they were nine and twelve respectively), some of them popular celebrities, such as Tom Cruise and Cher—have had a learning disability. It has been rumored that President George W. Bush had one too, which required his mother to go the flashcard route.

Although the law covers all children with special needs from birth, many children, especially those with learning disabilities, are not identified until later, although Granny-Nanny may suspect this is the case much earlier and, in his or her role as caregiver, can do a lot to get the process started. Those first three or four years of attention and love and understanding can be a real precursor to the professional help available in the classroom—which, incidentally, is getting better and more widespread every year.

Such services are free for qualified children, and, for the savvy, knowledgeable parent, referrals are not that hard to get. A great many advocacy and special education Internet sites have some very good, up-to-date info on this.

You will be amazed at what some states will do to fill the special needs of a schoolchild. For example, one school district determined that a deaf child would best be educated in a boarding school on the other side of the state. Each Sunday, a special ed bus driver would pick up the child and drive him to a midpoint in the state (a two-hour drive one way). There they would be met by a special ed bus driver from the boarding school's school district. The child would be transferred to that bus and taken back to school. Every Friday, the process repeated itself in reverse so that the child could spend weekends at home with his parents. It added up to sixteen hours of travel time (at time-and-a-half) for the bus drivers and the school districts. And the home school district picked up the tuition and the room and board. All this for just one child with special needs!

Coping With Anger, Grief, And Denial

A workshop for grandparents of disabled children held in Richmond-upon-Thames in England in 2000 brought to light many relevant issues. Many grandparents felt that just by being there they were playing an important role, and that they were acutely aware of and sensitive to the amount of input they should give without stepping on parents' toes.

In fact, a number of grandparents said caring for a child with disabilities had helped them to acknowledge their feelings about their special grandchild, to be more understanding, and to learn more about disabilities. Some suggested that having a disabled grandchild had brought the whole family closer together.

Here is what some of the grandparents attending the workshop had to say:

"It was hard coping and fighting . . . if only I had been ten years younger."

"I was very angry. Why our boy?"

"Hard to know how to support my daughter and her husband—tried to give them more space."

"Very difficult to accept. I wanted to help more."

"It was a double whammy—concern for the parents and also for the child."

Grandparents go through most of the same emotions as the parents when a child with disabilities enters their lives, including anger, grief, and denial. The initial reaction of all parties may be to look for something or someone to blame. One thing for sure, verbalizing such thoughts as "Whose side is to blame?" and "You can always have another child" won't help the situation one bit.

Advice To Grandparents Of Children With Disabilities

• Help the parents deal with the process of obtaining statutory services including health, education, and social services. It can be exhausting. Phone calls, support at meetings, and babysitting while these matters are being dealt with can be a big help.

• Talk to parents and grandparents of other children with disabilities to learn all you can from their experiences. Seek out support groups for the specific condition the grandchild has and get their literature and resource lists.

• Make sure the siblings don't feel left out because of all the attention the child with disabilities receives.

• Check to see if there is a grandparents' group in your area. They're not everywhere, but you may get lucky and find one. Or you could start one.

• If you can log on to the Internet, you can find chat rooms and forums for every conceivable disability. Start with Yahoo, which has, for example, over 1,000 individual discussion groups on autism, nearly 300 for asthma, just 10 for dyslexics, but 190 for attention-deficit problems. Although these can be very helpful, they're not quite the same as meeting face to face with someone dealing with a nearly identical problem.

• Accept the fact that your advice won't always be welcome.

• Do the little things parents will appreciate, such as babysitting so they can go out to dinner or a movie.

• If they need it now (and if you can afford it yourself), give them some of the money they are likely to inherit anyway later on.

Helping Others To Help Yourself

One story from the Richmond-upon-Thames workshop is worth repeating. The Coxes had helped to raise a handsome grandson whose autism was diagnosed at around three years. They had just recovered from that when a second grandson was born with multiple disabilities.

They began to ask why and ponder who or what was responsible. They dreaded the thought that some hereditary factor might be involved, and they suffered feelings of guilt. They continued to help care for the older boy and a sister (the youngest required full-time professional care), while at the same time learning as much as they could about their grandchildren's disabilities . . . and, more important, what they could do to help in this situation.

The children are now young adults, and the grandparents, who are in their eighties, live some distance away. They don't see the grandkids as often as they'd like, but they keep busy helping out at a club for people with disabilities, attending seminars and workshops on autism and genetics, and passing their knowledge on to needy parents and grandparents. These acts of participation and sharing have helped them come to terms with their own family situation, which started out being very upsetting and became more bearable with understanding and love. Best of all, it has helped them help others in similar circumstances.

A Wheelchair-Accessible Home

Children with physical disabilities call for a whole new way of thinking on the grandparents' part and make Granny-Nannying more of a challenge. Most homes are difficult to adapt for the wheelchair-bound: doorways may need widening, and ramps must be built to make the home accessible. Rather than spend a little on two homes, it is usually better to spend it all on the parent's residence, which means that Granny-Nannying takes place there.

But some grandparents choose to make their homes accessible as well so the disabled child can at least visit. So up go the ramps. Toys and learning aids are stored at the proper height so that a child using a wheelchair can reach them. Tables are elevated, if necessary, for the wheelchair arms to slide under. At least one washbasin is made reachable from the wheelchair. And easy-pass lanes need to be established from room to room.

One loving grandfather went to the trouble of renting a wheelchair and using it for a day so he could better understand his grandson's needs and feelings. Now there's a man after my own heart! I recommend this exercise as a necessary part of training for the parents and grandparents of children who are or will be using a wheelchair. In fact, there are all kinds of "ability awareness" programs out there that can help with understanding all types of disabilities.

Structure, Structure, Structure

Organization is very important for the child with disabilities. Specific places should be assigned where books, toys, homework, shoes, and other necessary items are always found and put back. That makes it easier for the child and the Granny-Nanny, too.

Likewise, children with disabilities need structure, structure, structure. They need to know what the rules are and how to follow them. It's not enough to tell them what not to do. Tell them and show them how you want them to behave. You may have to do this over and over again because children with disabilities may need extra time to follow directions. Your demands for a quick response can backfire, making the child angry. Don't expect children with disabilities to jump the minute you ask them to do something. They have to process your request, which can be a lengthy ordeal, and then they have to figure out how to comply with it.

Tell them and they will forget. Show them and they may remember. Involve them and they will understand. Have the patience for which we older citizens have become famous

Planning ahead is difficult for children with disabilities. They respond best to predictability and regular scheduling, so it's important to have things happen at approximately the same time and place. Give ample warning before you expect them to do something. Using pictures can help with scheduling. Then you can make changes to their schedules in a visual way.

One final piece of advice agreed upon by most specialists in caring for children with disabilities: don't "dumb it down" for the child. Challenge him or her. Modify the task if necessary, but encourage learning what it is, how to handle it, why it is important.

Reward progress with lots of hugs and kisses and hand-claps and cheers.

CHAPTER 21

Divorce Or Worse

Sometimes I lie awake at night, and I ask,

"Where have I gone wrong?"

Then a voice says to me,

"This is going to take more than one night."

—Charlie Brown

Although this isn't the last chapter in the book, it is the one I kept putting off and putting off. It is because there is so much potential anguish involved.

What could be worse than abuse? How about desertion, abandonment? Ask a child. He'll tell you that he can put up with abuse—so very many do—but to be abandoned, that's like dying.

Sometimes the abandonment is deliberate. Sometimes it's due to drugs. Sometimes it isn't abandonment at all, but departure due to outside forces.

Imagine this. You've been your grandchildren's Granny-Nanny for some time now and have gone through countless cries of "I want/miss my Mommy." The same with Daddy. And each time, you've replied, "Of course, you do," and quickly diverted attention away from the separation to something else.

Then, suddenly, one of the parents isn't there anymore. Maybe it's a short-term problem, such as an illness or an accident. Then, again, it could be something much more drastic such as call-up to military service or jail or divorce or even a death. What do you do then?

First, forget (or hide) your own feelings. Hard to do, I know, but your grandchildren need you to provide serenity and a safe place to go when their world is in turmoil and seems turned inside out and is just plain unfair. You have to provide a comfort zone where a grandchild can get away from a distressing situation, even if it's just for a little while. In other words, you have to be extra-calm and extra-accepting. And spend a lot of time diverting the young ones.

When Children Blame Themselves

Your next task is to provide reassurance. Children often feel that they're to blame for whatever has happened. For example, one child confessed that if she had only pooed in the toilet instead of her pants, Daddy wouldn't have gone away.

Seem farfetched? It isn't, not to immature minds. All the concentration on the child's toilet training had made the connection seem logical.

Another child blamed her father's decision to leave on her habit of biting her fingernails. She thought herself unworthy. So, she worked and worked and worked and broke the habit. She was so proud . . . but he didn't come back.

The point is that all of us, regardless of age, seek answers to why bad things happen to us or to the people we love. Swiss-born psychiatrist Dr. Elisabeth Kübler-Ross proposed that grieving (for any traumatic experience) involves five stages: denial, resentment, bargaining, depression, and acceptance.

For example, she applied her theory to divorce. One spouse wants it, the other doesn't. The latter refuses to believe or accept the possibility of a divorce...resents the disruption to his or her "I-thought-we-had-a-good-life" fantasy . . . bargains with the spouse to reconsider ("I'll join AA") . . . becomes depressed, and finally not only accepts the inevitable but begins some hard bargaining via lawyers. (I added that last bit about the lawyers, but you know it's true.)

When a traumatic experience such as divorce or death happens within a family, therapists have found that many in the family suffer from what is called survivor's guilt. In other words, an individual may feel guilty about failing to do enough for the deceased. What a person will remember is not the good things done, but things forgotten or neglected or left undone.

Young children, who up to the age of seven are very egocentric (everything is measured in terms of themselves), may feel even more guilt than older siblings or adults. They blame themselves and their actions for whatever has happened. They consider themselves at fault for deaths, divorces, separations, everything and anything bad.

It is up to the responsible adults to reassure children that they are not at fault for the temporary or permanent absence of a parent. Easily said (well, really easily said) in the case of a military call-up or an accident. But divorce destroys a child's world and may destroy the Granny-Nanny's as well.

Surviving Divorce

Let us say it's the daughter-in-law who wants the divorce. Is she going to want you to continue to Granny-Nanny? Not on your skinny, skinny skin. In fact, if she has another man on the line, she may not want you around, period.

Or take the reverse of that situation. Suppose the son-in-law wants the divorce and sues to get custody. Will he want you around as a constant reminder of the children's mother? Suppose there's joint custody, which is increasingly the case? Remarriage? Because there are so many combinations and permutations in marital and nonmarital relationships, there may be no blanket advice to give because each situation must be negotiated separately and with multiple parties. The bottom line is you may be out of a job as a Granny-Nanny, but never as a granny.

Grandparents' Rights

Which brings up what are probably the hardest-fought battles in family law: the grandparents' rights to visitation. The kids know you, they love you, their life has been hit by a tornado. They can use you. Maybe you can convince your daughter-in-law to let you babysit occasionally for her and her new man. The same applies to your son and his new wife.

Maybe they won't agree. The Grandparents Rights Organization (GRO, a nonprofit group that supports grandparents in this situation) is trying to get visitation rights passed into law in every state.

Several decades ago, visitation rights of increasing numbers of grandparents were being legislated out of existence because of family feuds. In response, grandparents joined together to get laws passed assuring them the right to petition for visitation in the case of parental death or divorce. One by one these laws were adopted, in various forms, until every state had one. Now, grandparents have the right to petition, but they still don't have automatic visitation rights in every state.

In a six-to-three decision, the U.S. Supreme Court decided in 2000 that grand-parents do not have an automatic right to visit their grandchildren. That decision was based on a Washington state case involving the grandparents of two sisters, ages eight and ten. The Supreme Court said a state law giving the grandparents visitation rights actually violated the U.S. Constitution. The Court held that as long as a child is not being harmed, the Constitution gives parents a fundamental right to raise their children without government interference. States like Michigan have passed laws attempting to circumvent this decision. But none, to my knowl-edge, has been tested in court. Therefore, grandparental legal rights remain in legal limbo.

What Does This Mean For You?

Walk gingerly and speak nicely to your grandchildren's parents. For example, the GRO suggests that you resolve to do the following:

- Don't use the children as pawns to hurt the other side/your son- or daughter-in-law.

- Tell the children that the divorce is not their fault, it's their parents' doing. Answer their questions together with the parents, if possible.

- Don't speak negatively about either parent or put the children in the position of having to take sides.

- Don't use the children to carry messages to the other parent.

- Don't bad-mouth the other parent so that children can hear it.

- Don't argue in front of the children.

- Include the other parent in school and other important activities.

- Encourage the relationship between the child(ren) and the other parent.

As for the parents, they should not attempt to cut a child off from his or her grandparents simply to get even with the other side. The GRO believes that if death takes a grandparent from a grandchild that is a tragedy, but if family bick-ering or vindictiveness denies a child the unconditional love of a grandparent, then that is a shame.

Legal Assistance

At this point, you may need help—legal help, that is.

One fight, as mentioned, may be over visitation rights . . . and in more drastic cases where, in your opinion, one or the other parent is unfit, you may be seeking custodial rights.

Prior to 1970, you, the grandparent, had absolutely no rights. Now all states have laws granting grandparents rights of one sort or another. Many are what is known as "restrictive," meaning that grandparents can get a court order for visitation only if the child's parents are divorcing, or if one or both parents have died.

If you want more, if you want custody or even to adopt, know this: your age will be held against you as compared to a cocaine addict. But if the parent is truly unfit, then you owe it to your grandchildren to intervene and to attempt to remove them from a bad situation.

So go for it. There are all sorts of places to start. The public library is one. Countless books have been written about grandparents as parents. The books offer good but limited advice, since most of the authors are doctors or child care experts or others in the same boat as you. Of more value would be a book written by a lawyer. I haven't found one, but books on the subject of custodial grandparents are being published every day.

Before you visit a lawyer, you might want to consult nolo.com, a website that has some very good answers about custodial grandparenting from a legal point of view.

I should warn you that, judging from the grandparents I've talked to who've gotten involved in this situation, there is no simple solution to the problem. If you get custody, you may still have to deal with the parent(s), which can be very unpleasant. Children involved in these battles can be traumatized and require all sorts of help; some may even resent you for interfering. I could go on and on, but I won't. However, if you decide to go the legal route, you might want to contact one or more of the following organizations. They may have literature on the subject. They may have names of lawyers who specialize in this area. They may be able to suggest an alternate approach to the situation:

• American Bar Association

• American Arbitration Association

• Academy of Family Mediators

• Conflict Resolution Centers

• Your local bar association (see Appendix 5, page 212)

For more information on your rights, Google the following organizations and agencies to find their websites:

• Grandparents United for Children's Rights, Inc.

• Grandparents Rights Organization

• Administration for Children and Families

• Nolo: Grandparent Visitation Rights

• American Academy of Family Mediators

• Lawyer Referral Services

• American Arbitration Association

• U.S. Department of Health and Human Services

• Generations United

• AARP

• Conflict Resolution Center

• American Bar Association

• Divorce Net

Resources By State:

• Divorce Source

• Children's Rights Council

You'll find their websites and addresses in Appendix 5, page 212.

Chat groups and forums on the Internet are invaluable in terms of hand-holding and propping you up emotionally during your battle for your rights. For example, go to Suite 101 (I may see you there) on Nurturing Grandparents (www.suite101.com/discussion.cfm/nurturing_grandparent).

In the meantime, let your child and grandchild know you are there for them. Tell them from time to time that your door is always open. Let them know you want them to come to you in good times and bad. As for your grandchildren, tell them you'll come and get them at a moment's notice, any time of day or night. All they have to do is call.

CHAPTER 22

Ending The Relationship

"For lack of better words,
I have to fire my mom.
I know she is great,
but her health is not, and
I don't feel very comfortable
now that he is
a very busy toddler!"

Sooner or later all good things come to an end. So does Granny-Nannying. The son or husband has gotten a big raise and Mommy can afford to stay home. Or maybe Mommy or Daddy hit the lottery—it happens—and Mommy and the kids will be rolling in luxury and want to send the Granny-Nanny on a trip around the world in repayment for all she's done.

We can all dream, can't we?

And, let's face it, we all want the children to be brought up by their mommies, not their grandparents.

And then—gasp!—there is always the possibility, not to say inevitability, of being outgrown. Yes, there will come a day when your nannikin will turn you into a Granny-Nanny has-been. Oh, sure, maybe he or she still comes to your house after the sports or activities buses drop them off, but now they're more apt to help you than vice versa. They have outgrown you. It happens around the age of twelve. Fortunately, it happens gradually, just as it did with your own children. Slowly but surely, children just simply outgrow Granny-Nannying.

But suppose there's another scenario. One in which the ending is more abrupt.

• Grandma may have become too infirm to handle the kids any longer, even though she may not think so.

• The parent may have grown tired of Granny-Nanny's constant meddling.

• Grandmother may be tired of all the back and forth with the kids and their diapers and clothing and food and toys and books and DVDs and you name it.

• Mother may be tired of encouraging, nay nagging, her elders into giving the children more physical activity time.

In which case, the parting is mutual, and all you have to do is consult your letter of agreement (see, I told you it would come in handy) and determine how much notice is required. Or waive notice, if it's convenient.

Padding The Parting Of The Ways

But suppose the parting is not mutual. How do you tell your mother or mother-in-law that her services are no longer wanted without hurting her feelings, or worse, causing a family rift?

How do you tell your daughter or daughter-in-law that you can no longer cope with her beautiful children? That you have sacrificed too much of what little time in good health you have left?

It's tricky.

Granny-Nanny Says Good-bye

To begin with, let's take the Granny-Nanny's modus operandi.

Don't Even Consider It . . .

It is the lowest-down, dirtiest trick in the world for a Granny-Nanny to *pretend* to quit just to prove her importance. Your daughter/daughter-in-law won't forgive you. Your grandkids won't forgive you. I and every other Granny-Nanny won't forgive you.

So What Are Valid Reasons For Giving Up Granny-Nannying?

1. Your health. The children are getting heavier and your joints are protesting the strain. You are concerned that you might drop one.

2. Your concern for the children's safety. If your hearing is going, your driving becoming erratic, your eyes getting blurry, and/or your memory shot, you are not doing your grandchildren a favor by caring for them.

3. Your nerves. Children are exciting and excitable. Maybe you were able to cope with one or two, but no more. When you have to start popping tranquilizers to get through the day until the children are picked up, it's time to call it quits.

4. You're feeling the pinch financially. I had an aunt who'd always say, "It's not convenient for us right now," when she meant "We are plain old flat broke and can't afford it." So, lay it on the line. Maybe the parents can help you out financially.

If your reasons are good and the well-being of the children paramount, your daughter or daughter-in-law isn't going to protest too long. One hopes for your ego's sake that she protests a while. If she says, "Yes!!!" before the words are barely out of your mouth, you know the situation wasn't working, and it's a good thing it's coming to an end. Let's hope she's more diplomatic than that. Perhaps she will come up with some alternatives to your quitting, like helping out financially. Maybe she will offer to pay for a cleaning service to free up some of your time. She may ask you to continue Granny-Nannying for a while so that she can make other arrangements. That's reasonable, and it is to your grandchildren's benefit that you agree. You don't want them in need.

For Parents Breaking The Bonds

But suppose it's the other way around. Suppose you are the daughter/daughter-in-law severing the relationship. This is going to call for big-time diplomacy if you hope to keep the family intact. Granny-Nanny is not going to be happy since no one—especially at the end of one's life—wants to be considered a failure. On the other hand, she may jump at the opportunity once she's given it some thought.

If the reason for dismissal is for some failing on Granny-Nanny's part, you'd better be prepared to phrase it as gracefully as possible and with as much gratitude and love as you can muster. You probably don't want to deprive your children of their grandparents' love and affection for the rest of the grandparents' short lifespan.

You'll be lucky if Granny says, "Wow, that's great. Now I can do all those things I've been waiting to do."

You'll be less lucky if she asks, "How can you tell the kids that someone else is going to take care of them instead of Grandma and Grandpa?" You'd better have a good answer.

How To Tell Your Granny-Nanny She's Going Back To Being Just A Granny:

1. Pick a good time to drop the word on her. Perhaps on a weekend after she's had a day to rest up and may be in a calmer, more receptive mood.

2. Do it, if possible, with both parents and both grandparents present. You want it to be a family decision, not a personal vendetta.

3. Don't deliver the news in front of the children. Tell them separately, after the fact, and in a way that won't upset the applecart.

4. Assure the grandparents that they'll still have access to the children and vice versa.

5. Tell them how much you have appreciated all the time and effort they have spent helping the children grow and learn and mature.

6. Offer Granny something nice—a day at a spa or a special framed picture of the kids—as a reward for her time and effort.

7. Be firm. Granny may put up some objections to being relieved of her duties. Don't let it escalate into an argument that could lead to a custody battle.

8. Live up to your agreements. If they're on paper, review them and make sure you've complied with all the stipulations.

How To Know When It's Time To Go . . .

So much for how to relieve Granny-Nanny of her role. But what are the signs that tell you, the parent, when it's time to make such a change? You can't just bury your head in the sand if there are problems. Your child's welfare is your top priority in this situation.

Burnout: Is your Granny-Nanny suffering from burnout? It's an all-too-common affliction in the child care profession. (You won't believe the turnover at child care centers.) The older she is, the more likely burnout will occur. Look for the signs. She may be putting off diaper changes, feeding snack foods instead of quality meals, not reading books to the children, not helping them learn, depending too much on the TV to keep the kids' attention.

Depression: It could also be that she is battling depression, zonked out on prescription medications, or not eating properly to maintain her stamina.

Problems with the kids: Watch for signs of interpersonal relationship problems between Granny-Nanny and her charges. It happens. For whatever reason, either the child takes a dislike to the Granny or vice versa. That's not a good situation, and in the extreme, it should be dealt with promptly.

Thin skin: If Granny-Nanny can't take criticism or suggestions without becoming upset or angry, you need to discuss whether she's willing to work on the problem. If she's not, then you must consider ending the relationship.

Follow-through: Is Granny following through on your letter of agreement (wave it under her nose if necessary)? No? Why not? Are her reasons reasonable or merely excuses? If the latter, it gives you a reason to invoke the termination clause.

Can't cope with older children: Maybe Granny was great with infants, but hasn't a clue as to how to cope with older children whose needs are totally different. Yes, she raised either you or your husband, but that was a long time ago. She's a much different person now—less active, less flexible, more set in her ways. If the wonderful world of the baby has turned into a chaotic circus for her, it's time to call it quits.

Whatever the cause, you can't let it interfere with the quality of care your kids need. Talking it through and suggesting a probation period may be an answer in less severe situations. Otherwise, cut the cord and get on with life.

Intuition: It's a terrific thing, especially in women. Men call it a gut thing. Women say it's a feeling, an instinct. If that instinct is shouting that something is wrong, if it's causing you worry and loss of sleep, there's probably something to it. Don't ignore it. Check it out and get the peace of mind you deserve.

Some Clues That Things Are Not As They Should Be:

• Watch for signs that your child is being abused verbally, physically, or sexually. Yes, even grandparents can be perpetrators, either without realizing it, or driven by motives they can't control.

• Look for marked behavioral changes in the child: more crying, indifference, agitation.

• Is the child suddenly reluctant to be with the Granny-Nanny, or is he eager to greet her? Fearful of adults? Afraid to be touched? Not wanting to have a diaper change? Heaven forbid it happens in your family, but if it does, take decisive action immediately.

• More telltale signs that something is afoul in your child care arrangement are your child's nervous mannerisms, extreme aggression, sleep problems, nightmares, bed-wetting after being fully potty trained, unexplained bruises, overdependence on comfort objects such as a stuffed animal or favorite blanket, and torn clothing.

Ending the Granny-Nanny role may not be easy for anyone. In the happiest circumstance, Granny will welcome the change. If not, do the tricky deed with compassion, firmness, a positive attitude, gratitude, a possible reward (however small), and the desire to maintain a good relationship for your sake and that of the children.

Remind her that she'll now have time to do other things, even write a book or memoir.

Granny, depending on the length of her service, will doubtless suffer some withdrawal symptoms ranging from needlessly waking at the same early hour to weaning herself from children's television. Sure, she'll soon begin to enjoy her newfound freedom, but those first minutes and days and weeks can be an adjustment.

Mommy, on the other hand, having been told to find someone else to take care of her kids, will be spending her every free waking moment trying to find good alternative child care. And working on a budget to determine what to squeeze and what to eliminate in order to pay for it.

All I can say is GOOD LUCK!

100 Years Of Child Care

Since the earliest days of human life,
there has been a Granny-Nanny fulfilling her role
as the designated child care provider in homes
where mothers had to work. But, during the
twentieth century, options for child care changed radically,
as did options for women in the workforce.

Pre-1940

In truth, before World War II, most women didn't work outside the home. Those who did—there were about five million of them—were mostly single, widows, or divorced. Some were fresh off the farm, but most had arrived from another country. They worked as servants or factory hands, for long hours, low pay, and frequently under intolerable conditions, either in the house or in the factory.

Whenever possible, the former farm girls or the new immigrants gravitated to areas where they had relatives or others with similar backgrounds. They lived many families to a dwelling, which kept the cost of rent down and allowed children to be cared for by in-home relatives.

This, by the way, was the forerunner of what is known in the twenty-first century as in-home family day care or relative care.

Not until World War II was there a true alternative to the Granny-Nanny as caregiver. Before that a working mother without other resources could lock her kids in a closet for the day, or, if a domestic, take her children to work with her. Or turn to the neighborhood "nursery" cited in Emily D. Cahan's *Past Caring: A History of U.S. Preschool Care and Education for the Poor, 1820–1965:*

> One woman occupying four dark, poorly ventilated rooms was crowding into them thirty or forty children each day; another was caring for twelve children in equally bad surroundings; a third, with less than one-tenth vision, was receiving fourteen children in her two rooms; and a fourth was caring for eight children whom she was in the habit of shutting behind locked doors on the second floor while she did her marketing.

What other choice did the working woman have? There was no Hobbit House, no Lighthouse Center, no ABC Center, no Play and Learn, no Above and Beyond, no Bizzy Bee's, no Huggable Center. . . nor any university-affiliated day care center nor community ones nor church-based ones—in fact, no day care centers as we now know them.

If you were rich, you had governesses and nursemaids and tutors. And if you were totally poverty-stricken, you also might be in luck. For you, there were charitable nurseries, patterned on the French crèches, established by wealthy women and philanthropists to save the children of poor working women from starvation and abuse. Sources differ as to when and where the first charitable nursery was founded, with estimates ranging from 1798 in Philadelphia to 1863, also in Philadelphia, with stops along the way in New York State.

In any event, when it happened was unimportant. What did happen was just short of earthshaking. Each new day care center was a success and inspired others to open them. But to send your child to one meant two things: one, you were accepting welfare and the social stigma that goes with it. And two, you were an unfit mother.

Yes, the blame game started decades ago, and its exponents were for the most part male (some things don't change, do they?). They were also self-taught experts in child welfare who pooh-poohed the need for day care. They thought motherhood a task doable only by mothers. And in a sense they were right. Except, they had identified the wrong mother. In the medium-income family, it was the mother of the mother—the Granny-Nanny—who provided the care when mothers had to go to work.

Enter Rosie The Riveter

As men marched off to battle in World War II, President Franklin Delano Roosevelt's defense production goals required the mass mobilization of women to work for the war effort. In a propaganda campaign orchestrated by the government, housewives morphed overnight into lunch-bucket-toting heroines. Rosie the Riveter[1] and her sisters donned slacks ("pants" referred to underwear) and flocked to factory assembly lines and shipyards to help in the war effort. But, in turn, the mothers in the group needed help. Help with child care. Help not quickly forthcoming as a battle raged between the child welfare professionals centered in the federal Children's Bureau and the representatives of war industries.

[1]"Rosie the Riveter" was the creation of artist-illustrator Norman Rockwell for the cover of the May 29th, 1943, issue of The Saturday Evening Post. The original oil painting (52 x 40 inches) was auctioned by Sotheby's on May 22, 2002 for $4,959,500.

"Where was a mother's place during the war?" asked Elizabeth Rose, associate professor at Vanderbilt University, in a speech given at the annual meeting of the Organization of American Historians in San Francisco in April 1997. "At a time when men were being conscripted for military service and civilians were being encouraged to sacrifice for the war effort, could mothers be called away from their normal duties to serve the nation as well? Child welfare advocates said no."

Experts such as Arnold Gesell, founder of the Gesell Institute, told a conference of the United Federal Workers of America that increased child care facilities were not the answer to the problems of working mothers. Rather, he argued, women must "be practical enough to hold to what was most important—the family." Gesell declared, "The family must get first and last protection—if the family goes, everything goes."

J. Edgar Hoover, director of the Federal Bureau of Investigation, concurred. He wrote, in an article entitled, "Mothers . . . Our Only Hope," that a mother "already has her war job. Her patriotism consists in not letting quite understandable desires to escape for a few months from a household routine or to get a little money of her own tempt her to quit it. There must be no absenteeism among mothers."

Talk about guilt trips!

Despite such remarks, by 1942, 60 percent of respondents in a National Opinion Research Center poll believed that married women should work in war industries.

Over the outspoken opposition of child welfare advocates, the Office of War Information (OWI) encouraged women to take up war work and asked popular magazines to present positive images of married women workers. Attacking the idea that the employed woman was an aberration in American life, writers and magazine editors sought to place her at the forefront of the public mind. Marriage and family responsibilities were not to be portrayed as a full-time career, but as fully compatible with the wartime duty to the country.

Convinced that day care was an effective tool for recruiting women employers, defense contractors like Curtiss-Wright in Buffalo and Kaiser Industries in Portland, Oregon, opened day care centers for their employees.

Conceding defeat, child welfare advocates spoke about setting up a foster parent network for children, but day care centers proved more feasible and popular with mothers. And some experts agreed. For example, day nursery activist Ethel Beer noted, "It may not be ideal for mothers to leave their homes to earn a living. But they do. That is why the day nursery exists . . . [It] is as sure a weapon as the gun on the battlefield."

The message of wartime propagandists was that women were supposed to take jobs out of duty and patriotism, not out of a desire to better themselves. Nor, if the truth be known, did they have to. According to a comparison published in *Barron's National Business and Financial Weekly*, April 24, 1944, families of soldiers and sailors were living quite comfortably on military pay.

> On the basis of expenditures for living by average families in different income groups—with deductions attributable to absence of the husband —the receipts of the buck private's family will enable its members to live according to standards prevailing among families with annual civilian earnings or income of $1,600. This tops the earnings or incomes of more than 50 percent of all the families in the country. And, during foreign service, his family's receipts may be measurably increased.

Now it may not seem like much to you, but in the 1940s this was living pretty handsomely, as the authors pointed out.

So, for most of the married mothers who went to work during the war, this was a golden opportunity to benefit their families. To save for the down payment on a new home. To get their children a better education. (All the same reasons that mothers go to work today and more. Today's mothers can also pursue a career simply because they want to.)

Simultaneously, they had the same concern that today's working mother has: her child's welfare. And many held the same belief that today's mother does: day care would be good for their children. For example, Mrs. K—, a 1940s mother, upon applying to a government-funded day care center, said her daughter had to learn how to get along with other children, and she felt it would be much simpler for other children to teach her this than for an adult.

Other mothers at the time echoed the same belief although at least one admitted that she had had a hard time explaining this part to her mother. Another woman said she thought it would be best for her family if she were able to go to work and leave her son in a place where he "could be associated with other children and where the adults around him would not have such a tendency to spoil him." She expressed the hope that maybe he'd even "learn to read and learn his ABCs" at the nursery.

Over and over again, mothers expressed the belief that a child can "gain a great deal from . . . group experience, learn social amenities and get a chance to develop." The idea that day care was beneficial for children as well as for parents thus bolstered women's perception that wage work was a good way to fulfill their family obligations and improve their children's future.

Between 1940 and 1944, an estimated five million women answered Rosie the Riveter's can-do rallying cry. And discovered they liked working. A Department of Labor survey reported in 1944 that 80 percent of American women wanted to keep their jobs after the war.

War work as a new opportunity for women was particularly meaningful for African-American women, who were able to earn higher wages and work in better jobs during the war than ever before. As one black woman said, "My sister always said that Hitler was the one that got us out of the white folks' kitchen."

Back To The Kitchen For You
When the war ended and the men starting coming home again, the forward movement of women into the workplace was thrown abruptly into reverse gear.

Even as women swore to keep on working, their share of the workforce in the next four years plummeted from 36 percent to 12 percent. Good-bye Rosie, hello Doris Day and June Cleaver…at least temporarily.

What happened? The GI Bill happened. On June 22, 1944, President Franklin D. Roosevelt signed the Servicemen's Readjustment Act of 1944, better known as the GI Bill of Rights. It granted GIs many things, including loans for houses. Suddenly, a young family didn't have to live with Grandma, or even near Grandma. They could move to "suburbia" and live in readymade "communities" (as they were labeled by the builders of Levittown and the like). Hundreds and thousands of almost identical houses ("crackerboxes" or "cookie-cutter houses," as many were called) sprang up out in the sticks—on acres of farmland away from everything, including relatives.

Thanks to the postwar "Baby Boom," most women retired from their jobs—many gratefully—to take up the role of mother in a brand-new house far away from family and friends.

But many others did not retire. For them, the need to work continued, and the closing of the day care centers shortly after the soldiers were mustered out of the military was a potential catastrophe. The mothers marched, they argued, they besieged city hall; they wrote letters to the editor, to politicians, to the President, to whomever they thought would listen.

Strangely enough, their argument was not based on the educational, developmental, and social benefits that they claimed day care gave their children. Instead public day care centers were defended on the grounds that they protected children from physical danger and juvenile delinquency.

The defenders were successful. Not in all states and not in all cities. But in some cities and states, day care centers continued to operate. And some universities began offering courses in preschool education, which eventually became degree programs.

Meet The Ms.

By the 1970s, many women no longer wanted to be identified by their marital status. Mrs. and Miss became Ms. The government had funded Head Start but restricted it to poor children. Women took to heart Betty Friedan's *The Feminine Mystique*, which postulated that women are victims of a false belief system that requires them to find identity and meaning in their lives through their husbands and children. Whether this new feminism was the cause or the effect, still more women entered the workforce, including more mothers.

To put women's contribution to the workforce in context, look at these statistics compiled by the U.S. Census Bureau:

- In 1900, 5.3 million women worked outside the home.

- By 1950, that number had more than tripled to 18.4 million.

- In 2003, the number had more than tripled again, to nearly 65 million.

- By 2010, the number of working women is projected to increase to 75.5 million.

Suburban mothers with neither close family nor public day care centers nearby turned to fellow suburbanites to form co-op day care groups. Shades of the squalid nurseries written about by Emily Cahan, you might think. But now, the surroundings were much cleaner, airier, and healthier than those of prewar days, although the staff were still nonprofessional, inexperienced women.

In the 1970s, women burned their bras and looked not just for work but for "careers" with a capital C. These career women, by and large, were not mothers. In fact, in 1970, according to statistics compiled by the AFL-CIO, 61 percent of children had mothers *who stayed at home full-time*.

However, another factor now came into play—professional day care centers began to appear, run by (mostly) women who were college-educated, like me. In Wisconsin, for example, it was estimated that:

- At the beginning of the 1970s there were 460 child care centers with a capacity for 12,600 children.

- Eight years later, there were 950 centers with a capacity of 29,209.

- In 2002, there were 3,088 family child care centers, 2,407 group child care centers, and 64 camps with a total capacity of 199,539 children!

One of the anomalies was that originally group centers greatly outnumbered the smaller family ones. But that changed in the 1990s as mothers became more critical, and as stay-at-home moms discovered they could augment their incomes by taking in other parents' children. It is now a full-fledged industry. One do-it-yourself day care start-up kit advertises that "you can earn $30,000 your very first year just taking care of neighbors' kids." The cost to you? A mere $19.95 for a book of instructions, menus, requisite forms, etc.

In any event, by the year 2000, 67 percent of children had mothers *in the paid workforce.* Or to put it another way, according to a telephone survey by Lake, Snell, Perry, & Associates, in 2002 nearly four of every five mothers of school-age children were in the paid workforce, as were 51 percent of mothers with infants under the age of one. "The speed of the change is astonishing," says Lynn Weiner, a dean at Chicago's Roosevelt University, who has written about the history of the female labor force.

Weiner is only one of many writing about this phenomenon. For example, books written specifically for the working mother have become a genre. They include *Working and Caring* by T. Berry Brazelton, M.D., the "Dr. Spock" of the late twentieth century; *Choosing Child Care for Dummies* by that parenting-book writing machine, Ann Douglas; and *She Works, He Works—How Two-Income Families Are Happier, Healthier, and Better Off* by Rosalind C. Barnett and Caryl Rivers. Surprisingly enough, after all those child welfare experts had spoken against it more than fifty years ago, all these authors now see no danger to the child, providing—always a proviso—the mother follows the author's advice. Another thing the books have in common is the premise that a mother's working is her choice—an option she could pursue or not, depending, again, on their advice.

What these experts do not acknowledge, possibly because they have never been in a similar situation themselves, is that somewhere along the line, most women lost that choice. For the first time in our lifetimes, middle-class women have to work.

Why? Because in the 1990s, two paychecks became necessary, according to the U.S. Census Bureau, just to maintain the standard of living the average single-income family enjoyed two decades earlier. Furthermore, it takes two incomes to afford the McMansions of the 2000s—a fact borne out by statistics showing that 80 percent of new houses purchased since 1990 were sold to two-income families.

What had happened between 1970 and 1990? Authors Elizabeth Warren and Amelia Warren Tyagi, in *The Two-Income Trap*, explain that this was the result of a "bidding war," in which parents were "competing furiously with one another for their most important possession: a house in a decent school district."

Things haven't changed all that much since World War II, have they? It is still the effort to improve a child's well-being that is the driving force behind many a mother's working and many a Granny-Nanny's devoted care.

Activities

The Great Indoors

Call it Cabin Fever, the Winter Blues, or the Summer Doldrums, but don't let 'em get you down. Takes a bit of doin', but the result is a happier grandchild and a lot less stress for Granny-Nanny. Countless activities can be undertaken indoors—at home or at the mall or a skating rink or another sports venue or at the movies or at a nursery or preschool. Let's begin at home.

Kitchen Companions

There's nothing like a cheery, warm kitchen to make a gloomy day brighter. Children as young as three can help you with cooking and baking.

Soft Pretzels

You will need:

- cookie sheet
- pancake turner or spatula
- wax paper or shallow bowl for sugar-cinnamon mixture
- microwave-proof measuring cup or saucepan for melting butter
- shallow bowl
- pastry brush (optional)
- parchment paper or grease-spray
- tongs for handling baked pretzels

Ingredients

- 1 package refrigerated unbaked breadsticks
- 1/4 pound butter
- 1/2 cup granulated sugar
- 1/2 to 1 teaspoon cinnamon (optional)

Note: Anything underlined, a child can probably do.

Soft Pretzels

- Preheat oven to 375°F.
- Line a cookie sheet with parchment paper or grease it or spray it.

Remove outer wrapper of breadstick package and whack carton against edge of counter. (Most kids like to do this, but may need to do it more than once.) Separate dough into 12 pieces. Fold each in half lengthwise (a little tricky for little fingers). Pull, shake, or stretch each piece of dough until it is at least 20 inches long. This is the fun part of pretzel making.

To shape dough into pretzel shape: Lay strip of dough down flat and bring ends toward you. Cross one end over the other about 6 inches up from bottom. Wrap that same end under its opposite, as if preparing to tie a knot. Holding both ends, bring them up and over the remaining dough like a pretzel. (Older children, once shown this, can do it for themselves.) Lift each pretzel with spatula or pancake turner and flip onto cookie sheet so that ends are underneath. I do not recommend children do the lifting and flipping unless you're prepared for flips, flops, and laughs.

- Bake for 10–15 minutes, or until golden brown.

While pretzels are baking, mix sugar and cinnamon on a sheet of wax paper or in plate or large shallow bowl. To apply topping, use either cold stick of butter like a crayon and roll across warm pretzel . . . or melt butter in microwave-proof cup and transfer to flat plate. You can dip finished pretzels in it using tongs or brush each with pastry brush.

- Dip buttered pretzel in sugar mixture using tongs.

Yield: Makes 12 probably lopsided but decidedly delicious soft pretzels.

If your grandchildren show an interest in cooking, take them to a bookstore and let them look through the children's cookbooks to see which one(s) appeal to them most. And then there are the Saturday afternoon food shows that follow *Sesame Street* and other children's programming on PBS, as well as the Food Channel, which might hold a child's interest. I know of one five-year-old who, on seeing a famous chef dish up an omelet, said, "Don't you think it needs some parsley on it?"

More Indoor Fun At Home

If you're desperate, ask your grandchild what he or she would like to do. If you get a shrug and "I don't know," suggest making a list. (If the child is old enough, the two of you can make separate lists and compare them. There may be things on your grandchild's list you never thought of trying.)

Possibilities: Jigsaw puzzles; painting wooden garden ornaments; playing cards, checkers, dominoes, or board games; wall stenciling; planting bulbs indoors; baking pretzels or cookies; making a scrapbook; writing; reading (see the list of books beginning on page 200); reorganizing collections; surfing the Internet; taking a bubble bath; watching movies; making popcorn; knitting something; making doll or baby clothes from pieces of cloth or tissue paper.

Need more ideas? Coloring; playing with dolls; rearranging Barbie and Kelly collections; playing board games; putting toppings on ready-to-bake pizza; painting wooden cutouts; making bead bracelets or key rings; doing a puzzle; playing dress-up; having a tea party; playing with the computer; brushing the dog or cat; putting nail polish on the child's toes; reading; swimming in the tub; cleaning house; making Mom a present; singing songs; taking pictures of pets; and watching TV.

Although it's great to do things together, we all need some time alone to do what we want, or just to pamper ourselves.

Bring The Outdoors Indoors

For more active things to do, if you have a long hall, children can ride tricycles or push-'em toys. We've even brought a plastic slide inside for the kids to go "whee" on. A friend with laminated floors in his family room says he lets his kids roller-skate in there. That's him, not me. How about you?

Mall Time

Malls offer an entire, contained world of games, distractions, enchantments, education, and nourishment (and non-nourishment). If you're near a mall, you'll see a parade of Granny-Nannies there on any rainy morning. Fortunately, many malls have strollers for free, including doubles and novelty strollers. And if the mall has a pet store, you can spend quite a bit of time just watching the animals playing in the window. Do not, however, make the mistake of asking, "How Much Is That Doggy in the Window?" Mom will never forgive you.

Indoors Away From Home

Aside from the mall, in the winter months, plan some indoor activities outside the home. Go to the market, visit a museum, bookstore, library (story hours are great), sporting event, movie matinee, or church social. Plan trips to local animal shelters, craft fairs, dog and cat shows, antique shops, and even a home show. Surprise, even the zoo has wintertime activities.

Summer offers more opportunities for fun activities out of the sun and in air-conditioned comfort. Bring in leaves and ferns to dry and preserve. Make a flower arrangement. Make popsicles, lemonade, or cotton candy.

Check your newspaper under family entertainment for lots of good ideas. Your local chamber of commerce or visitors bureau may also have a listing of current events that would be helpful.

The Great Outdoors

Outdoor activities are fun and good for both grandparents and grandchildren. But only if Grandma and Grandpa don't overdo it.

Brrrrrrr

In winter, the A-number-one thing to do in snow is **snow angels**. If you're able, show the kids how to fall backward in deep snow and move their arms up and down and their legs apart and together. The real trick is getting up carefully so you don't disturb the pretty angel pattern. I have been making them for decades and have never learned the secret of not leaving a trail. But maybe your grandkids can figure it out.

A little easier on your body is teaching children to **make disappearing trails:** have them make tracks in the snow by walking forward, and then have them walk backward, placing their feet in the same footprints.

Watch the kids giggle as they **catch snowflakes** on their tongues. It's tricky, but they'll soon catch on and really enjoy it.

Speaking of snow, **sledding** is great fun in the northern states or mountain areas. Granny-Nanny doesn't have to get on the sled, she can just pull toddlers on the sled or more modern snowboard, tube, or saucer. Take your grandchildren to a sledding/toboggan hill and take photos or video of them enjoying the ride. Use safety precautions with little children; make sure they know how to sit and hold on. Check the area they are sledding in for sticks, branches, stumps, or rocks they could hit. Too many hazards? Go to a safer hill.

The older grandchild may want to go **snowmobiling, snowboarding, skiing, or ice-skating.** Lessons and safety classes in these activities are a good idea, and the kids should be supervised, at least until they reach their teens. The hills and trails you pick should be designed for your grandchildren's level of skill or experience, and preferably where snow patrols are on duty.

Ice-skating is a favorite winter activity, with both indoor and outdoor rinks available in many areas. If you decide to venture out onto a pond, make sure the ice is at least six inches thick and is deemed safe by parks or rink officials. **Be alert to warning signs and stay away from restricted areas.**

You can help the kids make a snow fort if you live in a cold region. There are plastic forms that you can use to make blocks of hard-packed snow. Just stack the blocks to make a fort of any size or design. Use sandbox toys to make decorative touches for the fort. You can also create a temporary ice rink by making a circle with an old hose or lawn-edging plastic, filling it with water, and waiting for it to freeze. A word of caution: the rink may mess up your lawn come spring.

Walk around your house and scatter bread, cereal, or crackers for the birds and squirrels. Help the kids **build a snowman or a scarecrow.** Make a game of finding the right hat, scarf, mittens, broom, carrots, buttons, and throw-away clothing. Take pictures of your grandchildren hugging their creation. Then go inside and warm up with hot cocoa after making a snowman, or cool off with sweet cider when the scarecrow is finished.

Snowball wars are great so long as everyone understands that there is to be no hitting above the chest. Getting hit in the neck or face is no fun and can be dangerous. Better to set up a target and have the nannikins practice throwing snowballs at it. It's good practice for the upcoming baseball season. Rewards for scoring bull's-eyes will add fun and prolong the game. Some extra gloves and mittens might come in handy to avoid frostbite.

Taking a nature walk is good any time of the year. Photograph things you find interesting, like snow-covered trees, animal tracks, sunsets, birds, chipmunks, trees, clouds . . . just about anything. Keep a book with pictures of the constellations in the house, show it to your grandchildren, and, on a clear night, go outside for a few minutes and look up. The stars may be bright and the constellations easy to spot. Try to find Orion, the Big Dipper, and any others you can recognize. It really is a wonderland the kids should get to know and appreciate.

Warmer Days

In the spring there are early flowers to discover and birds to spy returning from their winter habitats. Time to put up some new bird feeders and put out some string and straw for nest-building. Time to fill the sandbox and repaint the playhouse. Time to get out the jump rope and the sidewalk chalk.

Chase butterflies (the child, not you). Find a duck pond or Canada goose hangout and feed the animals—but don't get too close. Throw the food into the water—never feed geese on land; they may come after you, and they can be vicious. Go for a walk in the park or take the kids to the playground.

Before you know it, summer has sneaked in and you can make a game of filling the wading pool and getting out the water toys. Bring out the hammock and the barbecue grill. If you have a regular swimming pool, you can teach the kids how to swim or dive (or at least float) in your pool. Or take them to a public or club pool where trained instructors can teach them swimming. Show them how to roast marshmallows over the grill. How to make a game of finding dandelion flowers. How to spot the weeds and get rid of them. TEACH THEM HOW TO IDENTIFY POISON IVY! Everything can be a game to the little ones. You just have to make it interesting.

Forward Into Fall

Fall presents a lot of new opportunities for fun with the grandkids. **Raking leaves into a pile and jumping in it** (not you—them!). Putting the leaves in trash bags. Making jack-o'-lanterns and scarecrows.

Sewing (or buying) costumes for Halloween. Closing up the sandbox and putting away the sand toys. Dreaming up a discovery game for Columbus Day. Putting out the flags and watching the parade on Veterans Day. Use your imagination. There are dozens of new challenges that will get you all the way through to the holiday season.

A FEW WORDS OF CAUTION

Do not allow children under eight to play outdoors unattended. They can fall, wander into the street, get into all sorts of yucky trouble. Older children should be checked on periodically, and you should always know their whereabouts. A little overprotection could save a life.

Of course you know not to let children play outdoors when there are blizzard conditions, or high wind-chill factors, or in the blazing sun without adequate protection. Most of all, use common sense. If it doesn't feel good to you, it can feel worse to the young ones.

Just what you've been waiting for!

A place for Granny-Nannies, parents, even grandchildren to ask questions, make comments, give advice, share experiences:

www.granny-nanny.com or www.grannynanny.com

Granny-Nanny Refresher Course

How quickly we forget what children can and should be able to do at various ages. This chart comes courtesy of the Child Development Institute (see Appendix 5, page 213). It is a source that I highly recommend.

General Developmental Sequence

Toddler Through Preschool

This section presents typical activities and achievements for children from two to five years of age. It is important to keep in mind that the time frames presented are averages and some children may achieve various developmental milestones earlier or later than the average but still be within the normal range. This information is presented to help parents understand what to expect from their child. Any questions you may have about your child's development should be shared with his doctor or teacher.

AGE 2

Physical Development

Walks well, goes up and down steps alone, runs, seats self on chair, becoming independent in toileting, uses spoon and fork, imitates circular stroke, turns pages singly, kicks ball, attempts to dress self, builds tower of six cubes.

Emotional Development

Very self-centered, just beginning a sense of personal identity and belongings, possessive, often negative, often frustrated, no ability to choose between alternatives, enjoys physical affection, resistive to change, becoming independent, more responsive to humor and distraction than discipline or reason.

Social Development

Solitary play, dependent on adult guidance, plays with dolls, refers to self by name, socially very immature, little concept of others as "people." May respond to simple direction.

AGE 2 (cont.)

Intellectual Development

Says words, phrases, and simple sentences, 272 words, understands simple directions, identifies simple pictures, likes to look at books, short attention span, avoids simple hazards, can do simple form board.

AGE 3

Physical Development

Runs well, marches, stands on one foot briefly, rides tricycle, imitates cross, feeds self well, puts on shoes and stockings, unbuttons and buttons, builds tower of ten cubes. Pours from pitcher.

Emotional Development

Likes to conform, easygoing attitude, not so resistive to change, more secure, greater sense of personal identity, beginning to be adventuresome, enjoys music.

Social Development

Parallel play, enjoys being by others, takes turns, knows if he is a boy or girl, enjoys brief group activities requiring no skill, likes to "help" in small ways—responds to verbal guidance.

Intellectual Development

Says short sentences, 896 words, great growth in communication, tells simple stories, uses words as tools of thought, wants to understand environment, answers questions, imaginative, may recite a few nursery rhymes.

AGE 4

Physical Development
Skips on one foot, draws "man," cuts with scissors (not well), can wash and dry face, dress self except ties, standing broad jump, throws ball overhand, high motor drive.

Emotional Development
Seems sure of himself, out-of-bounds behavior, often negative, may be defiant, seems to be testing himself out, needs controlled freedom.

Social Development
Cooperative play, enjoys other children's company, highly social, may play loosely organized group games such as tag or duck-duck-goose, is talkative, versatile.

Intellectual Development
Uses complete sentences, 1,540 words, asks endless questions, learning to generalize, highly imaginative, dramatic, can draw recognizable simple objects.

AGE 5

Physical Development
Hops and skips, dresses without help, good balance and smoother muscle action, skates, rides wagon and scooter, prints simple letters, handedness established, ties shoes, girls' small muscle development about one year ahead of boys'.

Emotional Development
Self-assured, stable, well-adjusted, home-centered, likes to associate with mother, capable of some self-criticism, enjoys responsibility. Likes to follow the rules.

AGE 5 (cont.)

Social Development

Highly cooperative play, has special "friends," highly organized, enjoys simple table games requiring turns and observing rules, playing "school," feels pride in clothes and accomplishments, eager to carry out some responsibility.

Intellectual Development

Tells long tales, 2,072 words, carries out directions well, reads own name, counts to 10, asks meaning of words, knows colors, beginning to know difference between fact and fiction/lying, interested in environment, city, stores, etc.

Age-Appropriate Books

(From the We the People Bookshelf, in cooperation with the American Library Association, and the National Endowment for the Humanities.)

Kindergarten to Grade 3
Either for reading by children or for reading to them.

Adventures of Pinocchio. Carlo Collodi.

Alexander and the Terrible, Horrible, No Good, Very Bad Day. Judith Viorst.

Alice's Adventures in Wonderland. Lewis Carroll.

All-of-a-Kind Family. Sydney Taylor.

Amelia Bedelia. Peggy Parish.

Anansi the Spider. Gerald McDermott.

Andy and the Lion. James Daugherty.

The Angus Series. Marjorie Flack.

Bedtime for Frances. Russell Hoban.

The Biggest Bear. Lynd Ward.

A Book of Nonsense. Edward Lear.

The Cabin Faced West. Jean Frit.

Caps for Sale. Esphyr Slobodkina.

The Carrot Seed. Ruth Krauss.

The Cat in the Hat. Dr. Seuss.

Charlotte's Web. E. B. White.

A Child's Garden of Verses. Robert Louis Stevenson.

Corduroy. Don Freeman.

The Cricket in Times Square. George Selden.

Crow Boy. Taro Yashima.

Curious George. H. A. Rey.

Fables. Aesop.

Frederick. Leo Lionni.

Freight Train. Donald Crews.

Frog and Toad Are Friends. Arnold Lobel.

The Garden of Abdul Gasazi. Chris Van Allsburg.

George and Martha. James Marshall.

The Girl Who Loved Wild Horses.
Paul Goble.

Goodnight Moon.
Margaret Wise Brown.

Harold and the Purple Crayon.
Crockett Johnson.

Harry the Dirty Dog. Gene Zion.

Leo the Late Bloomer. Robert Kraus.

The Little Engine That Could.
Watty Piper.

Little Toot. Hardie Gramatky.

Madeline. Ludwig Bemelmans.

Make Way for Ducklings.
Robert McCloskey.

Mike Mulligan and His Steam Shovel.
Virginia Lee Burton.

Many Moons. James Thurber.

Millions of Cats. Wanda Gag.

The Mouse and the Motorcycle.
Beverly Cleary.

Mr. Popper's Penguins. Richard and
Florence Atwater.

Paul Revere's Ride.
Henry Wadsworth Longfellow.

Put Me in the Zoo. Robert Lopshire.

The Reluctant Dragon.
Kenneth Grahame.

Sam the Minuteman.
Nathaniel Benchley.

The Snowy Day. Jack Ezra Keats.

Stone Soup. Marcia Brown.

The Story of Babar. Jean de Brunhoff.

The Story of Ferdinand. Munro Leaf.

Strega Nona. Tomie dePaola.

Sylvester and the Magic Pebble.
William Steig.

The Tale of Peter Rabbit. Beatrix Potter.

The Three Little Pigs. Paul Galdone.

A Tree Is Nice. Janice May Udry.

Watch the Stars Come Out.
Riki Levinson.

Where the Wild Things Are.
Maurice Sendak.

Why Mosquitoes Buzz in People's Ears.
Verna Aardema.

William's Doll. Charlotte Zolotow.

Winnie-the-Pooh. A. A. Milne

Grades 4-6

Anne of Green Gables.
L. M. Montgomery.

Ben and Me. Robert Lawson.

Betsy-Tacy. Maud Hart Lovelace.

Black Beauty. Anna Sewell.

The Black Stallion. Walter Farley.

The Borrowers. Mary Norton.

Bronzeville Boys and Girls.
Gwendolyn Brooks.

Bridge to Terabithia. Katherine Paterson.

Bunnicula. Deborah Howe.

Caddie Woodlawn. Carol Ryrie Brink.

Castle. David Macaulay.

The Children of Green Knowe.
L. M. Boston.

The Chronicles of Narnia. C. S. Lewis.

The Complete Fairy Tales ("Cinderella,"
"Sleeping Beauty," etc.).
Charles Perrault.

The Complete Grimm's Fairy Tales
("Hänsel and Gretel," "Rapunzel," etc.).
Jacob and Wilhelm Grimm.

The Dark Is Rising Sequence.
Susan Cooper.

Doctor Dolittle. Hugh Lofting.

The Dream Keeper and Other Poems.
Langston Hughes.

Half Magic. Edward Eager.

Fairy Tales. Hans Christian Andersen.

*From the Mixed-up Files of Mrs. Basil E.
Frankweiler.* E. L. Konigsburg.

Hans Brinker, or the Silver Skates.
Mary Mapes Dodge.

Harriet the Spy. Louise Fitzhugh.

Heidi. Johanna Spyri.

Hitty: Her First Hundred Years.
Rachel Field.

Homer Price. Robert McCloskey.

The House of Dies Drear.
Virginia Hamilton.

The Jungle Books. Rudyard Kipling.

Lassie Come Home. Eric Knight.

Little House on the Prairie.
Laura Ingalls Wilder.

Mary Poppins. P. L. Travers.

The Matchlock Gun.
Walter D. Edmonds.

Misty of Chincoteague.
Marguerite Henry.

The Moffats. Eleanor Estes.

Mrs. Frisby and the Rats of Nimh.
Robert C. O'Brien.

My Side of the Mountain.
Jean Craighead George.

The Phantom Tollbooth. Norton Juster.

Pippi Longstocking. Astrid Lindgren.

Prydain Chronicles. Lloyd Alexander.

The Pushcart War. Jean Merrill.

The Railway Children. E. Nesbit.

Rascal. Sterling North.

The Rescuers. Margery Sharp.

Rip Van Winkle. Washington Irving.

Roller Skates. Ruth Sawyer.

Sarah Plain and Tall.
Patricia Maclachan.

The Secret Garden.
Frances Hodgson Burnett.

Strawberry Girl. Lois Lenski.

The Summer of the Swans. Betsy Byars.

Swiss Family Robinson. Johann Wyss.

Tales from Shakespeare.
Charles and Mary Lamb.

Thimble Summer. Elizabeth Enright.

To Be a Slave. Julius Lester.

Tom's Midnight Garden. Philippa Pearce.

Tuck Everlasting. Natalie Babbitt.

The Wind in the Willows.
Kenneth Grahame.

The Wonderful Wizard of Oz.
L. Frank Baum.

Grades 7–8

Across Five Aprils. Irene Hunt.

Adventures of Sherlock Holmes.
Sir Arthur Conan Doyle.

Adventures of Tom Sawyer. Mark Twain.

The Bridge of San Luis Rey.
Thornton Wilder.

Call It Courage. Armstrong Sperry.

Call of the Wild. Jack London.

A Christmas Carol. Charles Dickens.

The Count of Monte Cristo.
Alexander Dumas.

Daddy Long Legs. Jean Webster.

A Day No Pigs Would Die.
Robert Newton Peck.

Diary of a Young Girl. Anne Frank.

Dragonsong. Anne McCaffrey.

Dragonwings. Laurence Yep.

Enchantress from the Stars.
Sylvia Engdahl.

The Endless Steppe. Esther Hautzig.

Fahrenheit 451. Ray Bradbury.

Frankenstein. Mary Shelley.

The Ghost Belonged to Me.
Richard Peck.

Goodbye, Mr. Chips. James Hilton.

The Hobbit. J. R. R. Tolkien.

The Horatio Hornblower Series.
C. S. Forester.

The Hunchback of Notre Dame.
Victor Hugo.

Incident at Hawk's Hill.
Allan W. Eckert.

Island of the Blue Dolphins.
Scott O'Dell.

Ivanhoe. Sir Walter Scott.

Jacob Have I Loved. Katherine Paterson.

Johnny Tremain. Esther Forbes.

Journey to Topaz. Yoshiko Uchida.

Julie of the Wolves.
Jean Craighead George.

Kim. Rudyard Kipling.

The Last Mission. Harry Mazer.

The Last of the Mohicans.
James Fenimore Cooper.

Le Morte d'Arthur. Sir Thomas Malory.

The Legend of Sleepy Hollow.
Washington Irving.

The Little Prince.
Antoine de Saint-Exupéry.

Little Women. Louisa May Alcott.

The Merry Adventures of Robin Hood.
Howard Pyle.

My Friend Flicka. Mary O'Hara.

Narrative of the Life of Frederick Douglass. Frederick Douglass.

National Velvet. Enid Bagnold.

The Outsiders. S. E. Hinton.

The Pigman. Paul Zindel.

The Pilgrim's Progress. John Bunyan.

Poems. Robert Frost.

The Red Pony. John Steinbeck.

Rifles for Watie. Harold Keith.

Robinson Crusoe. Daniel Defoe.

Roll of Thunder, Hear My Cry. Mildred D. Taylor.

Shane. Jack Schaefer.

Story of My Life. Helen Keller.

A Stranger Came Ashore. Mollie Hunter.

Treasure Island. Robert Louis Stevenson.

A Tree Grows in Brooklyn. Betty Smith.

20,000 Leagues Under the Sea. Jules Verne.

The Upstairs Room. Johanna Reiss.

War of the Worlds. H. G. Wells.

Where the Red Fern Grows. Wilson Rawls.

The White Mountains. John Christopher.

The Witch of Blackbird Pond. Elizabeth George Speare.

A Wizard of Earthsea. Ursula K. LeGuin.

A Wrinkle in Time. Madeleine L'Engle.

The Yearling. Marjorie Kinnan Rawlings.

And let me add one: *Whale Talk* by Chris Crutcher. This is a treat for adults and children alike. In fact, you can't be too old to enjoy this.

Granny-Nanny Benning's Recommendations For Pre-K Kids

This is an annotated list of the books my own prekindergarten grandchildren have loved. Some of the books are even interactive.

Undersea Open Sesame, by Kees Moerbeek.

The book has a tendency to come apart, but it goes back together easily. Kids love revealing the sea things hidden inside.

First Words, a Leap Frog book.

One of those lift-the-flap books that help children learn to identify objects. It's been around a long time—the telephone in it has a dial, not push buttons. Kids love the flaps although, in truth, some of them are a little weird.

Good Night, Gorilla, by Peggy Rathman.

This is probably her most popular. Children love the fact that all the animals have toys. And the mouse with its banana is fascinating. But you won't go wrong with anything by Peggy Rathman: *The Day the Babies Crawled Away*, *Officer Buckle and Gloria*, and *Ten Minutes 'Til Bedtime*, which just happens to be my favorite.

Nursery Rhyme Funtime, illustrations by Gil Guile, no author given, Book Studio.

It has tabs that one pulls to reveal parts of the nursery rhyme. A little hard for young fingers to work, but they love to watch Humpty Dumpty crash and go back together again.

Spot's Noisy Walk, by Eric Hill, a Play-A-Sound Book.

I include this against my better judgment. Requires batteries—grrrr! It's irritatingly noisy. But the kids play with it over and over again, which may be why I'm not so fond of it.

Busy Fingers 1 2 3, A Touch and Learn Book, Silver Dolphin Books.

No story to it, requires "reader" to keep asking how many this and how many that, but the nannikins never seem to get tired of it.

Who's Hiding in the Jungle?, Paragon Publishing Book.

A lift-the-flap book which, no matter how many times they lift the flaps, always seems to surprise them.

Goodnight Moon, by Margaret Wise Brown.

Maybe the quietest, most serene, gentle classic that has ever held children mesmerized.

Mr. Brown Can Moo, Can You? by Dr. Seuss.

If you can moo or make any of the other sounds, children are fascinated. When it comes to the horse clopping, the nannikins love to slap the page to imitate the clopping sound.

Brown Bear, Brown Bear, What Do You See? by Bill Martin Jr.

This is one of those books that the children won't look at for weeks, and then want to have read to them over and over again.

In a People House, by Theodore Le Sieg.

"Come inside, Mr. Bird," says the mouse . . . and you and the kids are off on a rhyming tour of a very old-fashioned house with some rather unusual objects in it.

Look and Find Books. There are a gazillion of them, ranging from pretty basic to so complicated even adults can't find the hidden objects. Actually, that's a cop-out—I can't find them. For the youngest children, between two and three, the Disney Princess book is very simple and clean and lovely. Nemo is good, too. All the Pooh books, Pooh, Tigger, Eeyore, every single one of them. These are excellent "run-your-finger-down-the-page" eye-training books that help children learn to go left to right. Who knows, it might help with a dyslexic child.

Those based upon the Disney princess movies are much more complicated, but older children will like them.

How Do Dinosaurs Say Good Night?, by Jane Yolen, illustrations by Mark Teague.

This was one of those carry-around books that had to be pried out of little hands. (Interestingly enough, the Scholastic Video of the story is not a favorite. In fact, they prefer not to watch it. I suspect the dinosaurs are too realistic.)

Barnyard Dance, by Sandra Boynton.

This is not a put-'em-to-sleep book since nannikins love to act it out.

Fidgety Fish, by Ruth Galloway.

If you can bbbbuuuurrrrrppp or whooooooosh, the kids will adore it.

Bunny My Honey, by Anita Jeram.

This is an especially good book for nannikins because it is so reassuring: bunny finds her mommy!

Excuse Me . . . Are You a Witch? by Emily Horn.

It was introduced pre-Halloween and is still going strong months later. What the kids like about it is that it is told by a cat, and it talks about people. Such as, I am informed, Nana and Pop-Pop.

Dragon's Merry Christmas, by Dav Pilkey.

Four short stories so you can stop after one, two, or three. What they like about it is that the dragon does nice things.

The Little Engine That Could, by Watty Piper.

You can actually see by the kids' body language that they're helping that engine up the hill . . . and the relief when it comes down again. A classic, of course.

A final word on classic fairy tales. Most of them are too bloodcurdling for pre-K children. Especially anything with doglike wolves that act very undoglike . . . as in "*Little Red Riding Hood*" and "*The Three Little Pigs*."

Age-Appropriate Toys
As recommended by the American Academy of Pediatrics

Use these recommendations when shopping for toys. Keep in mind that these are only guidelines. All toys can be dangerous when they are not used properly or are in poor condition. Parents should continue to watch out for mislabeled toys and always properly supervise young children.

Newborn To One-Year-Old (Baby)
Choose brightly colored, lightweight toys that appeal to your baby's sight, hearing, and touch.

1. Cloth, plastic, or board books with large pictures

2. Large blocks of wood or plastic

3. Pots and pans

4. Rattles

5. Soft, washable animals, dolls, or balls

6. Bright, movable objects that are out of baby's reach

7. Busy boards

8. Floating bath toys

9. Squeeze toys

One- To Two-Year-Old (Toddler)
Toys for this age group should be safe and be able to withstand a toddler's curious nature.

1. Cloth, plastic, or board books with large pictures

2. Sturdy dolls

3. Kiddy cars

One- To Two-Year-Old (Toddler) (continued)

4. Musical tops

5. Nesting blocks

6. Push and pull toys (remember, no long strings)

7. Stacking toys

8. Toy telephones (without cords)

Two- To Five-Year-Old (Preschooler)

Toys for this age group can be creative or imitate the activities of parents and older children.

1. Books (short stories or action stories)

2. Blackboard and chalk

3. Building blocks

4. Crayons, nontoxic finger paints, clay

5. Hammer and bench

6. Housekeeping toys

7. Outdoor toys: sandbox (with a lid), slide, swing, playhouse

8. Transportation toys (tricycles, cars, wagons)

9. Tape or record player

10. Simple puzzles with large pieces

11. Dress-up clothes

12. Tea party utensils

Five- To Nine-Year-Old Child

Toys for this age group should help develop new skills and creativity.

1. Blunt scissors, sewing sets
2. Card games
3. Doctor and nurse kits
4. Hand puppets
5. Balls
6. Bicycles with helmets
7. Crafts
8. Electric trains
9. Paper dolls
10. Jump ropes
11. Roller skates with protective gear
12. Sports equipment
13. Table games

Ten- To Fourteen-Year-Old Child

Hobbies and scientific activities are ideal for this age group.

1. Computer games
2. Sewing, knitting, needlework
3. Microscopes/telescopes
4. Table and board games
5. Sports equipment
6. Hobby collections

Resources

For Help And Hand-Holding

GrandsPlace

Here you are going to find more information than you'll know what to do with: legal, financial, emotional.

154 Cottage Rd., Enfield CT 06082

Phone: 860-763-5789

Fax: 860-763-1568

E-mail: kathy@grandsplace.com

www.grandsplace.com

Grandparents Rights Organization

The largest support group for grandparents in the nation.

100 W. Long Lake Rd., Suite 250

Bloomfield Hills, MI 48304

Phone: 248-646-7177

Fax: 248-646-9722

www.grandparentsrights.org

Generations United

GU includes more than 100 national, state, and local organizations representing more than 70 million Americans and is the only national organization advocating for the mutual well-being of children, youth, and older adults.

Generations United (continued)

1333 H Street NW, Suite 500 W

Washington, DC 20005-4752

Phone: 202-289-3979

Fax: 202-289-3952

www.gu.org

E-mail: gu@gu.org

AARP Grandparent Information Center

601 E Street NW

Washington, DC 20049

Phone: 888-OUR-AARP

(888-687-2277)

Fax: 202-434-6474

www.aarp.org/life/grandparents

The Baby Center

Unfortunately only available on the Internet, but to access this advice, it's almost worth buying a computer. It has all sorts of information – from when girls are ready for pierced ears to ideas for party games.

http://parentcenter.babycenter.com

For Expert Opinions

American Academy of Child & Adolescent Psychiatry

3615 Wisconsin Ave. NW
Washington, DC 20016-3007
Phone: 202-966-7300
Fax: 202-966-2891
www.aacap.org

American Academy of Pediatrics

141 Northwest Point Blvd.
Elk Grove Village, IL 60007-1098
Phone: 847-434-4000
Fax: 847-434-8000
www.aap.org

Child Development Institute

An excellent source of information, particularly for the disadvantaged child . . . and for the Granny-Nanny who suddenly finds herself wondering how to handle homework help.

3528 E. Ridgeway Rd.
Orange, CA 92867
Phone: 714-998-8617
www.childdevelopmentinfo.com

LEGAL HELP

Nolo: Law for All

For definitions and explanations of terms concerning child care, go to:
www.nolo.com and search for "grandparents"

Nolo: Law for All (continued)

950 Parker St.
Berkeley, CA 94710-2524
Phone: 800-728-3555
Fax: 800-645-0895

American Bar Association

740 15th St. NW
Washington, DC 20005-1019
Phone: 202-662-1000
Dispute resolution:
dispute@abanet.org
General info: askaba@abanet.org
www.abanet.org

American Arbitration Association

Customer Service
335 Madison Avenue, Floor 10
New York, NY 10017-4605
Toll Free: 800-778-7879
Fax: 212-716-5907
E-mail: Websitemail@adr.org
www.adr.org

Association for Conflict Resolution

1015 18th Street NW, Suite 1150
Washington, DC 20036
Phone: 202-464-9700
Fax: 202-464-9720
www.acrnet.org
E-mail: acr@acrnet.org

Setting Up A Child Care Center

National Child Care Information Center

NCCIC partners with the Children's Bureau, U.S. Department of Health and Human Services, as a clearinghouse and information source on child care. This is the place to go for everything, and I do mean everything, you need to know to start and run a successful child care center.

10530 Rosehaven St., Suite 400 • Fairfax, VA 22030

Phone: 800-616-2242 • Fax: 800-716-2242 • TTY: 800-516-2242

www.nccic.org

Email: info@nccic.org

Information On Child Abuse

National Clearinghouse on Child Abuse and Neglect Information

Children's Bureau, Administration for Children and Families, U.S. Department of Health and Human Services.

330 C Street SW • Washington, DC 20447

Phone: 800-394-3366 or 703-385-7565 • Fax: 703-385-3206

http://nccanch.acf.hhs.gov

E-mail: nccanch@caliber.com

For crisis counseling, contact: Childhelp USA® 800-422-4453

To subscribe to its e-mail list, go to:

http://nccanch.acf.hhs.gov/admin/subscribe.cfm

Tennyson Center for Children at Colorado Christian Home

This Colorado-based organization has great tips for everyone interested in preventing child abuse and neglect.

www.childabuse.org

Online Sources For More Information

(These sources are for informational purposes only. They are not recommendations of the author.)

1. All American Nanny

Nationwide placement agency guaranteeing live-in nannies for at least a one-year term. DMV, criminal, and medical checks on all nannies.

www.allamericannanny.com

2. Fisher-Price

Read parenting advice from experts at Fisher-Price.com.

www.fisher-price.com

3. World Vision

Become a child sponsor through World Vision and help break the cycle of poverty in communities worldwide.

www.worldvision.org

4. AuPairCare

Full-service au pair agency regulated by the U.S. Department of State.

www.aupaircare.com

5. Bright Horizons

Provider of work-site child care, early education, and worklife consulting services.

www.brighthorizons.com

6. Nannies4hire

Online nanny referral service.

www.nannies4hire.com

7. Child Care By The Hour Start-Up CD

For those interested in starting their own child-care business.

www.stay-working.com

8. CCVillage

Early childhood resource for day care providers, preschools, and parents. Art projects, music, movement, activity sheets, business forms, menus, and more.

www.ccvillage.com

9. Procter & Gamble

Child-care products as well as tips for the family.

www.pg.com

10. GoNannies.com

Online resource for nannies and other domestic personnel.

www.gonannies.com

11. La Petite Academy

Early childhood education and care for infants, toddlers, and children.

www.lapetite.com

12. Maternity Card

Resource for information on how to handle the costs of having a baby.

www.maternitycard.com

13. KinderCare Learning Centers

Provider of child care and preschool education.

www.kindercare.com

14. Children's Hospitals and Clinics of Minnesota

Information on children's illness, treatments, procedures, and medicines.

www.childrenshc.org

15. Shopping.com

Thousands of online stores.

www.shopping.com

16. Quadro

Indoor play centers for preschool-age children.

www.quadrozone.com

17. Overstock.com

Online resource for books, movies, music, and gaming titles.

www.overstock.com

18. TeacherCare

One-on-one, in-home child care and enrichment program for newborn through school-age children.

www.teachercare.com

19. ChildrenFirst

National provider of corporate-sponsored backup child care.

www.childrenfirst.com

20. Tummytime, Inc.

Record baby's activities and milestones in a keepsake journal.

www.tummytimeinc.com

21. SOS Children's Villages

An international child welfare organization providing long-term care for orphans and children in need.

www.sos-childrensvillages.org

22. NannyBackgrounds.com

Pre-employment background checks for the child care industry.

www.nannybackgrounds.com

23. The Felt Source

Flannelboard sets, felt puppets, games, and more.

www.thefeltsource.com

24. VMS, Inc.

Books, videos, and software packages from producers of instructional materials.

www.vms-online.com

25. FEI Behavioral Health

International Employee Assistance Programs and Crisis Management.

www.feinet.com

26. Verybestbaby.com

Information on child care, pregnancy, and new motherhood from Nestlé Infant Nutrition.

www.verybestbaby.com

Child Care Accreditation Services

- The Council on Accreditation of Services for Families and Children, Inc. (COA)

- The National Child Care Association (NCCA), the trade association of the for-profit companies

- The Preschool Accreditation Program of the Association of Christian Schools International (ACSI)

- The Ecumenical Child Care Network (ECCN) of the National Council of Churches in Christ (in cooperation with the NAEYC)

- National Association for the Education of Young Children . . . excellence in early childhood education

  1509 16th St. NW, Washington, DC 20036
  202-232-8777 • 800-424-2460
  webmaster@naeyc.org. • www.naeyc.org

NAEYC administers a national, voluntary accreditation system to help raise the quality of all types of preschools, kindergartens, and child care centers. Currently there are nearly 9,000 NAEYC-accredited programs, serving more than 760,000 children and their families.

- National Association For Family Child Care

- National School-Age Care Alliance

If you wish to learn more about licensing and accreditation, visit the website of the National Resource Center for Health and Safety in Child Care (NRC), and go to the individual state child care licensing regulations section. It gives you the full text of each state's child care regulations for centers and family homes—if regulated, and many aren't. School-age child care and mildly ill child care facility regulations are included if applicable to an individual state. Contact information for each state's licensing office is also included under the state listing.

EduCare program, for accrediting au pairs

If you have Internet access and want more information on the au pair EduCare programs, go to:

exchanges.state.gov/education/jexchanges/private/aupair_brochure.htm

Acknowledgements

There is no possible way that I can thank everyone who helped on this project. Besides which you know who you are. So, forgive me for singling out a few:

• Gloria Mosesson, who saw in this subject something worthwhile. And The Cleveland Clinic, which agreed with her. Larry Chilnick, who mentored it; Judy Knipe, who word-doctored it; Whitney Campbell, who whipped it into shape; and Kathy DeLong, who brought a fresh perspective to the whole thing.

• Gay Hoff, who shared so freely her twenty years of schoolbusmanship.

• **The Spillane ladies:**

Jean Spillane, who provided me with nannikins and made Granny-Nannying a delight.

Anne Spillane, who saved my bacon when it came to children with disabilities.

Elizabeth Spillane, who shared Granny-Nanny duties so I could write this book.

• Georgianna (Gan) Mears, who worked like a Trojan in lining up resources.

• The many, many mothers who chose to remain anonymous—Tina and Jean were the exceptions. And the Granny-Nannies who did the same, again with three exceptions: Helen and Nonnie and Noonie.

- Caroline G. Hauser, Director of St. Thomas' Nursery School, who kept me going in a straight line.

- Kathryn Grant Ellman of KGPR, who gave me permission to quote from BabyCenter.com.

- Leslie Ogilvy for medical assistance.

- Fidelia Notman, Income Support Programs, Child Development and Care, State of Michigan—a good state for grandparents to live in.

- Lisa Blaney-Koen, Senior Managing Editor, Medem Inc., who helped guide me in the right direction.

- Richard S. Victor, PLLC, who gave me permission to quote the "pledge" from the Grandparent Rights Organization, which he founded.

- "Eddie in Tampa" with the Social Security Administration, who explained how payments to Granny-Nannies can affect their Social Security checks.

- Kay Hollestelle of the Children's Foundation.

- Jennifer Caccamo of the English Nanny & Governess School, who clued me in on the differences between nannies and governesses.

- Suzanne W. Helburn and Barbara R. Bergmann, whose book *America's Child Care Problem: The Way Out*, which I heartily recommend, was of immense help. Speaking of books, I consulted nearly one hundred of them in researching this topic. I suggest you save your time and money; most are of little or no use to parents and grandparents who are sharing child care.

- Sallie Campbell and her grandson Tanner Johnson, for their candid picture of playtime at grandma's on page 29.

- And lastly, to my hands-on teachers of Granny-Nannying: Emma, Paige, and Tara.

Cleveland Clinic Press

The Cleveland Clinic Press is a full-line publisher of non-fiction trade books and other media for the medical, health, nutrition, and exercise markets. Our fall-winter list includes the Cleveland Clinic Guides and our new hardcover imprint, Crile Books.

It is the mission of the Press to increase the health literacy of the American public and to dispel myths and misinformation about medicine, health care, and treatment. Our authors include leading authorities from The Cleveland Clinic as well as a diverse list of experts drawn from medical and health institutions whose research and treatment breakthroughs have helped countless people.

Each Cleveland Clinic Guide provides the health-care consumer with the highest quality, practical, useful, reliable, and authoritative information. Every book is reviewed for accuracy and timeliness by the experts of The Cleveland Clinic.

Crile Books focus on serious medical issues that confront society, with stories of medical drama and important biographical studies of the leaders in medical science and health care.

www.clevelandclinicpress.org

The Cleveland Clinic Foundation

The Cleveland Clinic Foundation is one of the largest, not-for-profit multi-specialty group practices in the United States and is recognized as a world leader in the diagnosis and treatment of cardiovascular disease.

Since 1995, *U.S. News & World Report* has ranked The Cleveland Clinic Heart Center as the "Best" provider of cardiac care in America for 11 consecutive years. In 2002, The Cleveland Clinic Heart Center performed 3,825 cardiac surgical procedures, substantially more than any other center in the U.S. Of those procedures, 520 were minimally invasive valve repairs/replacements with a 0% mortality rate, again representing the largest subspecialty practice in the nation. The Cleveland Clinic Heart Center performed 60 heart transplants in 2002, and its overall mortality rate for all cardiac surgical procedures was 2.0%.

www.ccf.org

Cleveland Clinic Press

9500 Euclid Ave. NA32
Cleveland, OH 44195
216-444-1158
www.clevelandclinicpress.org